Wo
Lock

A collaboration of stories by
Lisa Li and other Authors

Lisa Li

ISBN : 9798720118303

Cover Artwork by Marco Poma & Paola Lucrezi
Edited by Dianne Custance

This book is dedicated to every reader with their own story, looking out from their own window.

For Nan (and Pup) x

CONTENTS

INTRODUCTION

On 23 January 2020, the Central Government of China imposed a lockdown in Wuhan and other cities in an effort to quarantine the centre of an outbreak of coronavirus. The world suffered a domino effect as the virus spread and many countries handled things in their own unique ways.

The UK lockdown began on on 16 March 2020, when MPs told the House of Commons that all unnecessary social contact should cease.

Over the course of 2020, thousands have died, businesses and schools have closed and the world turned upside down, and for a long stretch of time a lot of us were in some kind of isolation. Here is a book of collected stories from around the world to show some of the journeys and perspectives individuals have experienced during the **World in Lockdown**.

...Book first published exactly one year on, 16 March 2021.

LISA LI, 37 UK

When videos started pouring across the internet from Wuhan China, I was in shock. Panic set in hearing of this deadly virus, seeing bodies dropping to the ground… people sharing information, horrific scenes… Fear, disbelief !!

Being extremely sensitive I can see now how I was moving through a wave of collective terror… I couldn't think straight, I was just feeling EVERYTHING … My PTSD triggered – attack, mistrust, doubt, conspiracies being spread faster than any plague cold or flu. It knocked me off my feet, my instincts were to protect my family… to warn them, to advise them, to know everything. It took over me, much to the annoyance of many family members, I'm sure...

A warrior at heart, it's not news to me that we are run by a society that does not necessarily have our best interests at heart. Health care systems I had shunned after a childhood of popping pills for lung conditions, and the patriarchy I had long escaped. I was living like a pirate, travelling the world since my teens pretty much, dodging responsibility – if responsibility meant working a 9-5 and being miserable and knackered.

Many years I had travelled the world seeking solace on empty beaches, in jungles and within communities where I didn't even understand the language.

Everywhere I went I met beautiful people, and spent time with so many cultures… not from the usual tourist track, but from within the homes and at the tables of people who made me feel like family.

I had learned to meditate… an absolute game changer, then later on breathwork and other healing modalities, that helped me to dive even deeper into my body to unlock the traumas of my life.

I realised thru study I was most probably carrying PTSD from a forceps birth, this is where a baby is pulled out with metal tongs from the softest part of its head – what a great idea !!
I was certain I had needed extra support as a child that I of course didn't receive. Who knew how you are born could affect your life.

I read so many books and studied so hard… not with the intention of teaching this, but with the hope I could figure out how to feel better !! My sister would roll her eyes at my "self improvement" books, but she had no idea of the pain I was constantly living in and I didn't really talk about it with anyone.

Healing was not cool or fashionable back then… It was just something I had to do.

The last years I had taken all that I had learned and put it into a healing workshop called the breath ceremony. I had been travelling now sharing this work, often in the healing areas of huge festivals. Sometimes hundreds of people all lay down breathing and healing together, it was powerful.

I enjoyed this… It gave me a purpose and freedom, and loved the opportunity to help people… But I was still lost. I just didn't know where I belonged. I imagined one day opening a healing centre by a lake, maybe in Guatemala…who knows, I was sure the path would become clear one day, wouldn't it ??

What I didn't realise was… for the path to start to appear… I had needed to be still.

So, at the end of 2019 after another long summer driving around European festivals… I finally came back to my hometown. I had decided to stay near my grandmother, who was pretty old at this point. With my family scattered across the globe, I felt it my duty to be close to her. I started dating my childhood sweetheart, who had appeared in a dream a couple of weeks before landing back in the UK. I hadn't seen or even thought of him for 20 years and just like that, had this magical connection once more. I had grounded and rooted myself down beside the very river I grew up by, just in time for what broke out in 2020.

Magic had already started happening. It was as if the universe was conspiring to get me exactly where I needed to be. Everything led me back home and fell into place, supporting me to be there ready and waiting. Amazing really.

It was interesting to me... who of my travelling friends had ended up in their home countries… and who had been stuck elsewhere – I couldn't help but feel that everything was perfect and happening as it should.

Lockdown for me, once my initial panic had subsided, was actually pretty normal… Apart from starting to do my weekly shopping late at night away from the crowds, nothing too much had changed.

But honestly, it was the fear the people carried that I was avoiding more than the virus. I knew how stressed people made me feel, and so I avoided that at all costs.

I couldn't really understand everybody's decisions… people seemed to be getting their knickers in a twist complaining, yet choosing to go peak hours standing in supermarket queues. Also watching the news incessantly, which drilled in further how scared they needed to be. Didn't they realise how what you feed your mind will affect how you feel?

I was suddenly thankful for all my years of meditation.

In my world, the birds were still singing... we still continued to walk with the dogs in the same hidden spots in the countryside as before... and I started to work from home via zoom, and had loads of time alone... Nothing new there, but being in the UK for the whole year, now that was different.

I had fled from my town in middle England long ago, still in my teens I started to run. I remembered nothing but violence and stressful confusing situations growing up. I had picked up a weed habit very young to numb from all the emotional pain, and had developed an ego, so tough to keep people at arms-length, to make up for my small size, I guess. It saved me from many an ass kicking I'm sure... but was not so easy to drop once I found myself in a less violent space and out of the wildness and unpredictability of a childhood in that rough town.

Years went by and I stayed away mostly, only visiting my family a couple times a year… It was enough. Walking through the town centre gave me huge anxiety back then, and my relationship with my parents was still volatile. But year after year, the more healing I did, we eventually created a strong bond and I was able to spend more time in England.

My parents had moved to Turkey the year previous to my return and we now had a very good relationship. They still had an apartment in my hometown which is where I had landed and made home before and during lockdown. I felt so thankful for this I can't even express.

With trauma, memories and emotions can be stored deep inside the body for decades, until the body is in a safe enough space to process. This is why we end up still carrying the wounds of our childhood – unless we take the time to go back and unpack it.

And now it seemed I felt safe and supported enough and had all the time.

My love fed me big home cooked meals on repeat. We joked at what a feeder he is... definitely the way he shows he cares. His house was cold as he thought central heating to be unnatural, so sleeping there brought out all kinds of sickness from my body. The cold has a detoxing effect I was learning. I had sickness on repeat the months before Covid hit, yet it was making me much stronger. Some nights my body would just convulse, shaking and releasing stored trauma.. By the time Covid came I had never physically been so strong.

We were madly in love... We had so many memories from when we were younger to process. The connection we had was just as powerful as when we were teenagers. We didn't realise how much us splitting had affected us – we were so young.

Turned out we both had a deep love for nature… he had 2 dogs and we spent many days walking across the back fields and burning fires in forgotten woodland. This was truly magical to me, how he knew the land so well. And I still saw him as that cheeky wild boy who made me laugh and fall in love in an instant.

Even though I had immersed myself in so much incredible nature around the world… I hadn't really ever appreciated fully the beauty of my home country, England.
Spending so much time outdoors, we saw endless birds of prey, we went camping out beneath the sounds of woodpeckers high up in the trees… I'd only ever heard those before in Guatemala!!

And we even saw 2 robin red breasts doing an actual mating dance, right there on a fence in the middle of the council estate. We couldn't believe our eyes !!

We were in paradise, we barely remembered there was a pandemic going on and how scared we were meant to feel.

I was not so secretly loving lockdown. It meant I had nowhere to go, no plans to make, nothing to achieve, no pressure to be doing anything, but just allowing myself to BE.

We got chickens, we camped on the beach…

And with all that love i was feeling – For this world and for the future… I chose to be a lighthouse and not to join in the storm. Since the beginning I had been holding breath ceremonies online on the full and new moons… I was holding a safe space, and supporting others to go through their processes… Yet behind the scenes, as always in life, things were not all sunshine and rainbows.

We triggered the hell out of each other.

Some say it's called Twin Flame, this kind of relationship. Where you are drawn together like magnets, and both although, deeply in love, can't help but shed light on the others deepest wounds. We triggered each other… HARD. So much love was there, but without processing all the triggered emotions, one could easy build up a lot of resentment for all the pain it seemed that the other had caused.
Yet, I knew, this was healing us greatly.

We would spend weeks together and then weeks apart, licking our wounds and learning our lessons.

He was showing me my weaknesses, and me his.

It was hard to let it go in the end… He wasn't as fast to heal and learn (so I thought) but truth was he reflected back so many of my own unconscious issues.

The inability to let go of control, the pride to be right, bitterness that I realised I was still carrying for the past and all that I'd been thru. Still carrying it as some sort of shield to protect me from it happening again, yet this "protection" left me unable to fully move forward in my life.

I could see it so clear in him... but it took me a good while to see this in myself.

As the weeks went on… I let all this new awareness tear me apart. And I realised we weren't killing the love – we were killing each others shadow… and how beautiful that was.

This kind of relationship cannot exist without truth.

We were done with the old ways of relating, and our personal drive for awareness just would not allow it.

So I let go, and I loved,

I loved my new inner freedom… my passion for life… and all the energy and creativity that was starting to flow beyond all that pain I had released.

I had found myself... FINALLY.

And even some land with a lake appeared right on my doorstep… from my old manifestations.

Now if you had told me 5 years ago that I'd be living in England and loving it, I'd have told you to get your head checked. But it is true !!!

And I've realised that it truly doesn't matter where you are, or who you're with, its how you feel...

And you can move to the furthest place on earth, and chase the endless sunshine, but your unresolved past will follow you right there.

I had to heal at my roots.

To finish, one of my favourite quotes…

"No man ever steps in the same river twice, for it's not the same river and he's not the same man."

— Heraclitus

I believe that not one of us are the same after swimming the rivers of 2020.

And that gives me hope for change.

x

DIANNE, RETIRED UK CITIZEN IN SOUTH CHINA SEA

On a cold winter's day in January 2020, Paul and I flew away from England and looked forward to the hotter climate, guaranteed in Cambodia. We had been there several times in the past, visiting our son, Gary, who has lived there for several years. We were particularly excited about this trip, as we were going to meet Gary's partner, Narann and her daughter, Chona for the first time. We planned to spend a week with him and his new family and then, as in previous years, move on to experience a new adventure in other nearby Asian countries.

Before we left England, we'd already heard the news of the new virus, that was tearing through China. But we had no qualms about taking our trip. We weren't going to China, so why worry! They'd had similar, weird epidemics in the past and we'd never had to be concerned before. It never entered our heads to give it a second thought!

However, when we arrived in Phnom Penh, we followed our son's advice and went out to buy face masks, surprised to find that the shops there were already in short supply. Not many people seemed to be concerned about the virus so whilst there, the masks remained tucked away in our hotel room. We spent our time happily cut off from news, from the rest of the world and oblivious to the start of the spread of Corona Virus.

After six wonderful days, we had to say goodbye to our son and his family. We were sad to leave them but, as the plane took off, we cheered up and looked forward to landing in Thailand and a one night stopover in a luxury hotel. As we arrived at the Shangri-La Hotel, we were met at the entrance by a young hotel representative, who greeted us warmly and explained that he had to take our temperatures. Whilst checking in, we quickly learned that the Thailand authorities had started monitoring for any unwelcome signs of the Chinese virus infiltrating their country. But still, at this point, we didn't realise how deadly the virus was, or how quickly it was spreading. We remained optimistic and looked forward to joining our cruise the following day.

Our driver collected us from the hotel, just before midday, and we set off to join our Silver Seas ship, the Silver Spirit. In 2019 we'd sailed on that same ship and looked forward to settling back into its luxurious setting and our lovely suite. Arriving at the port of Laem Chabang for the usual booking in process, we were a little surprised that they didn't take our temperatures. But, instead we were asked about our health and had to complete the normal health questionnaire, with a few extra questions, relating to the Corona Virus. We felt confident that, once on board, we could forget all about the epidemic in China and relax for the next two weeks on our trip to Hong Kong.

With a glass of champagne in hand, I sat in reception, waiting for Paul to collect our suite door passes. The room was crowded and noisy with fellow passengers happily taking in their surroundings. As Paul returned to me with our passes, he looked a little unsettled. It wasn't long before the conversations in the room were mainly directed onto the same subject. Hong Kong had closed its port to all cruise ships with immediate effect! The Corona Virus had arrived there and was already taking its toll on its citizens. So, for the next hour or two we had to make contact with our lovely holiday advisor, Janet and organise a very different ending to our trip. We'd been looking forward to our first time in Hong Kong, where we'd booked a hotel for three nights and a later flight back home. Janet quickly organised a flight home from Manila, the capital of the Philippines, which the Captain had decided would be the ship's final destination. Janet reassured us that she would deal with getting refunds from the hotel and the flight booked from Hong Kong. So, just a little disappointed, we concentrated on what would still be a wonderful trip.

For the following two days we remained at sea, as we sailed towards Ho Chi Minh in Vietnam. The weather was glorious, the food delicious, as usual, and all we had to do was relax – read books, sunbathe and enjoy a few cocktails. What more could we ask for! We had a two day stopover in Vietnam and enjoyed a day in the city. We'd been there before, so we spent the other day lounging about on the swimming pool deck. We felt very safe and comfortable on board our floating hotel, where, even without any virus lurking on the horizon, it was expected that the clientele would regularly use the hand sanitisers everywhere you ventured on board. It goes without saying, really, that we were very pleased to avoid Hong Kong and the terrible virus that had reached its shores.

We spent the next two days, again, at sea as we sailed towards Romblon in the Philippines. From now on, our days would be filled with excursions - planned regularly each day, as we docked at a different port almost every day. On the second day at sea, we were enjoying a cocktail after lunch, when the Captain's voice echoed around the ship. It was bad news. Romblon was not allowing cruise ships to dock. At this point there was a lot of speculation amongst our fellow passengers and we fled to our suite, feeling disappointed as yet another destination was cut from our itinerary.

Whilst we changed for dinner, we broke our silence with the outside world and listened eagerly to the television news channels. A cruise ship in a Japanese port had cases of Corona Virus on board amongst the passengers. It felt a little disconcerting, but everyone on board our ship was in good health - to the best of our knowledge! We shrugged off any niggling worries and went off to enjoy our dinner. What else could we do? Hopefully the rest of our destinations would be happy to let us in.

So, we sailed past Romblon, hoping to be allowed into Coron, the third largest island of the Philippines. Another day went by only to learn that, even though we were 'virus free', our ship could not dock at Coron. It wasn't long before our distraught Captain informed us that Kaohsiug and Keelung in Taiwan were no longer happy to sanction a visit from our ship. This just left Manila - from where we had tickets ready for us to fly home. But no, the whole of the Philippines had closed their doors on us and we couldn't even fly home from there. The Captain's voice came back on the airways, asking all passengers to meet in the theatre at 6.30 for an emergency meeting.

The theatre was packed. Everyone was disappointed. A few were quite alarmed and worried about our prospects for getting home. But, the champagne flowed and we all tried to make the most of our time, floating around on the South China Sea. We felt a little better, as he told us his plans - to turn the ship around and head back to Vietnam, where the authorities had reassured him that we could all disembark and fly home to whatever destinations we chose. Even better, he confirmed that we would all receive a full refund for our cruises. I think the Captain was relieved that he didn't have an angry crowd to deal with.

By this time we had been at sea for about three days since leaving Ho Chi Minh. We settled in for a further three days sailing back. There were no signs of illness on our ship, so everyone made the most of the facilities. We had quite a lot of 'on board money' to spend, so I made the most of it and went for a relaxing massage and the following day had my hair and nails done.

We were getting closer and closer to Ho Chi Minh, when the bomb shell hit. Vietnam had closed its port to us. Cruise ships were not welcome. The Captain tried to sound upbeat, as he told us that Thailand would still allow us in. By now we were not feeling confident and chatted with our new friends about the dilemma that kept getting worse. Everyone was placing bets on where we would try next IF Thailand rejected us. Several people thought we might aim for the

Mediterranean and possibly dock in Italy. That seemed like a likely scenario. Little did we know!

A further two days at sea were now required to reach Thailand. There was another meeting with the Captain in the theatre, where he told us that Silver Seas would now take over making all arrangements for our flights home. No one needed to worry about organising anything. We just had to turn up the following morning to discuss details of where we wanted to go. His request for 'Any questions' was met with, 'if we're turned down by Thailand, how long will our fuel last?' and quickly followed by, more importantly, 'how long will the champagne last?' Everyone laughed! We had nothing to fear. We would neither starve, nor die of thirst!

Seven days earlier than our wonderful cruise was originally due to finish in Hong Kong, we left the Silver Spirit in Thailand and set off on our journey home. We'd had some anxious moments when our flights weren't finalised until the last possible minute and worried that we might end up stranded in Thailand. We were so relieved when we arrived at Bangkok airport, where we heard that our ship was the last one allowed into the port, before it closed its doors to any more desperate travellers. We had survived without a single person on board going down with the Corona virus - but we now understand the fear and concerns from all the various ports that had turned us away - they did the right thing - just in case!

We wore our face masks in Bangkok airport and all the way home on the plane. I felt a little anxious, as there were quite a few coughs and nose blowers on board. And, I have to admit that, on that last morning on board, I had woken up with a sore throat and tickly cough too. I worried all the way home that I'd now got the virus. We knew by then that the virus was spreading fast across the world and expected some serious checking to be done, once we landed in the UK at Heathrow airport. But no, there was nothing! No temperatures taken. No health forms to fill in. No questions...

Just to be on the safe side, the following day, I called 111. I was feeling pretty sick and had had a very bad night. Within a few hours I had an appointment at our local hospital, in a separate isolation building and had a test for the virus. I was told to self-isolate for 14 days, during which time I would receive the results to the test. Lucky for me it came back negative, but it took about 10 days to reach me. We were certainly the lucky ones and our commiserations go out to all the unfortunate people, whose cruises turned into real nightmares, with the Virus rife on board.

Our story is not a tragic story; nothing like what so many people have lived through in 2020. But, it isn't an experience I'd want to go through again. As so many places turned their backs on us, it made me think of all the refugees in the world and how they must feel as they flee from persecution with nowhere to go. No-one to offer them a safe haven. And, we are now safe at home. Lockdown is easy for us. We should all grumble less and remember those less fortunate than ourselves.

SHERYLE, RETIRED AUSTRALIAN CITIZEN IN BALI.

The year was 2020. It is now early 2021 and 2000 words were requested by my youngest daughter in Germany, on my experience during Covid! In two words: Sufferable and insufferable!

How my husband and I tempted fate with a discussion not long before Covid hit us! That we have been lucky in our 60s to have lived through some good decades. The fabulous 60's to 90's. The music, the cars, the clothes, the inventions etc, without pestilence or war coming to families, unlike our parents, grandparents and great grandparents before us.

Then in 2020 came the COVID pandemic to our shore, Australia!

What is the COVID-19 pandemic?

The COVID-19 pandemic, also known as the coronavirus pandemic, was and is an ongoing pandemic of coronavirus disease 2019 (COVID-19) caused by the transmission of severe acute respiratory syndrome coronavirus 2 (SARS-CoV-2), which was first identified in December 2019 in Wuhan, China. The outbreak was declared a Public Health Emergency of International Concern in January 2020, and a pandemic in March 2020.

As of this day Sunday, 21st of February 2021, there have been reputedly 111 million cases, 62.4 million recovered and 2.45 million deaths worldwide. I say reputedly for a reason, that I will elucidate on later.

Where was I when I first heard of this illness that spread dread and panic throughout the world?

I was on a relaxing holiday in Bali with my eldest daughter and her sister in-law. When on holiday I take my mobile only for that rare check-up with home, or emergency situation. After all, I am on holiday AWAY from everyone and everything for a while. No disruptions unless of absolute importance, PLEASE!

My daughter and her sister-in-law on the other hand are of the age where signing a mobile phone contract is more binding than marriage. You know, "Till death do you part" never to be divorced from their mobile.

We had been in Bali for a couple of days, when our mobiles rang with important news from our husbands!

"There is a new disease spreading around the world called, 'Covid'. People are being advised to wear surgical masks. In the Australian supermarkets people are panic buying, stocking up on tinned food; especially fighting over toilet rolls. There is talk that the government is considering shutting down airports". SO, with that news ringing in our ears like the toll of doom, we did what any sensible person would do! We said to our husbands, "Well, get up to the supermarket and get some canned food and some toilet rolls for us, in case people panic and empty the shelves". Seriously!

I thought to myself, "Thankfully we are returning home in a couple of days' time". If they decide to shut the airports, we may be impounded and stranded for who knows how long. Things may get worse, before better!

Now, I absolutely abhor panic! It scares me! I try to keep a cool head. A stiff upper lip and all that! Suddenly the enjoyment of an idyllic break of shopping, eating out and basking in the hotel pool was compromised, violently endangered, dramatically combusted. Both my ladies, worried, discussed, dissected the situation and gnawed ad nauseum on the bone of "Covid".

I spent some time considering outcomes and commiserating, before my verbal exchange with them became no more than pesky flies!

I realised my thoughts and advice of, "Let's not panic and enjoy instead the few days we have left, before we have to swim in the vomit bucket that is Covid. We've advised home what to do. We can't do more while stuck here". We're as useless as used toilet paper to them. The sky was falling!

Not to be restful the remainder of our holiday, for now our peace was suddenly and unexpectedly shattered crystal. Words of enjoyment now replaced with a diarrhea of incessant concern, into their mobiles. Instead of the hotel pool, we were suddenly swimming in the slimy morass that was to be an ongoing litany of fear and worry. I followed their refrain of confusion, as it poured over me sweeping away any efforts of holiday calm and peace before it. Damn!

So it began. We wonder sometimes, don't we, when we see an End of the World film. Just what would happen if we couldn't be with our loved ones. If we couldn't get home in time?

Well here we were not home, peace shattered, as Covid gnawed away at our serenity and peace. How serious is this? Will family get ill? Heaven forbid! How many people will die?

I tried not to think, not to go there. Covid was not going to manipulate me until I got home! I'd come for a holiday and wanted to relax and enjoy it, as if this was to be my last supper! No one really knew what to do, what was happening or what was going to happen.

Heaven knows when, or if we'd have the opportunity to holiday again, or if we'd ever return to Bali!

A couple of days' later, we flew home! On govt advice people returning from overseas must isolate in their home under quarantine for 14 days. We each did the right thing and isolated. Adults were advised face masks were mandatory if leaving the home to buy essentials. Visitors and visiting was banned.

Economies were soon affected. People were required to stay home from work unless essential services. Businesses, doctors, dentists, medical, schools etc closed, except for emergencies. Livelihoods were being shattered, as many lost opportunities, their business, jobs or support structure. Attitudes affected by the fear and misery not only of Covid, but of being now unable to afford their mortgage, rental or car repayments, etc. To support their family or themselves as they are used to.

The scary humans with aggressive self-preservation attitudes soon appeared! People started treating others as if they had the plague! Not respecting others or being rude in their demeanour! Some too scared to even say hello behind their masks! In the 70's, I remember the Aids epidemic. Govt ads on tv advised, "You could all die, whole families!" It sent people into panic. They became angry, some vicious. Most of the information we found out later was misinformed!

During Covid some Govts offered monetary and other support for those hit hard. Yet many hundreds of thousands worldwide will not recover financially or even emotionally! Then there was the ongoing question and indeed arguments put by many. "Were people actually dying in such huge numbers, or was this a trick, or manipulation by Governments"? Was people's trust being manipulated? Why if the govt couldn't afford to house people, build hospitals, do medical research before Covid, did they suddenly find billions to invest in supporting people and financing the research needed to roll out effective Covid drugs?

The news stated the government told the vast majority of infected people to go home, as most infected people developed mild to moderate symptoms and would recover without hospitalisation. How then were listed number of deaths in the millions?

There was the concern of many that govts actioning Covid drugs to protect against the disease, would make them mandatory instead of personal choice.

Due to the fast-paced research and actioning, will the drugs used be safe in the long term?

2020 moved on like a tortoise in a race that finished like a hare. I wore my mask, walked the dogs, went to the supermarket (they were allowed to stay open as an essential service). Many businesses and shops were closed on government advice. As were many airports, to prevent the spread of the disease. Stay home was the perpetual warning! Be safe!

So, I read copiously as I do anyway, but with more a sense that I have time, not having to rush to go somewhere, or do something. Time slowed like melted chocolate and the taste was sweet to my soul! The world was shutting down in its effort to contain the spread of the disease. People started to realise just how much we had been impressed by this hurry, hurry, worry, worry world.

I did hobbies, manipulated my computer and manhandled my mobile. Like many I spent money online shopping because the mail was STILL being delivered! How long would this lockdown last? At least for the foreseeable future, so why save? What for? Our future was no longer written in holiday travel brochures.

I ate, more of the naughty foods than I should. Most people locked in put on weight, as potato chips and ice-cream, chocolates, cakes, bread became comfort food.

Life can be short. No promise of a long life. Some of my friends and relatives had passed too soon. Covid was a wakeup call!

People watched the news; Not a pastime of mine. The reports, the negativity, the pain! Do you know anyone who has died? How many? Where? Who is not taking this seriously? Who is doing the wrong thing? Who do we believe? Is there subterfuge? Abuse, rage, fear! Regurgitate, regurgitate! Ignorance be my peace!

My husband argued throughout with everyone! Especially me; raised his voice and demanded Covid is all a ruse! I tired of the discussion. I hated the word "Covid".

I began to suffer with locked in syndrome. The bed was unmade, the floor at times un-mopped. No-one was able or coming to visit! My zest became withered disillusion.

We had not heard ambulances and people advised that the local hospital, and ambulances were mostly sitting at peace in their bays. No people we knew of were affected. Those on the news mainly spoke out upset at losing an elderly parent to Covid. Yet somewhere thousands of people had and were dying!

How does one measure the accuracy, or inaccuracy of words and worldwide reports, for people crave the negativity and depravity of bad news more than the good. It makes the tumultuousness of their own life seem less, to hear of others struggling more.

News is money. It drives the wheel of commerce and industry. It controls and manipulates. It is the pied piper of our reality today.

It is situations such as Covid where we see who the weak and manipulative are amongst us. Those that put themselves forefront. That would save themselves at the cost of others. It is also a time when we realise who is of strong and true heart. The people who work and care. Who share! It's in these times of concern that we notice acts of altruism and the kindness, of intelligent humility and humanity.

It is February, 2021, and our families and friends have come through relatively and luckily unscathed. Not so sadly, for the many reported in the news. Some limitations have been reduced or lifted as less cases are reported.

People are now able to leave their homes and shop in the stores permitted to open. Rushing to fill every spare moment with self-enjoyment. Covid has made us aware that life and lifestyles end. We have one chance to make of it what we can, and people released from worry are now in overdrive!

We put our trust in politicians, in experts. How do we cope when actions and reactions are controlled, or taken out of our hands by organisations or governments? When we are advised there is a big, bad wolf out there?

We buckle down. We look around at what we have to appreciate. We live in hope that we are being treated with a modicum of respect, protection and fairness and amidst that, we seek to enjoy any crumbs of peace and contentment.

Covid is a wakeup call, as with any life threatening, harmful action of our life. We assess, reassess and set ourselves on the path of survival.

The question most important now, is can, or when, will Covid be absolutely controlled? When will we be freed from this calamity and await with bated breath for the next?

DAVID, 30 MEXICO

Luckily I can consider myself very lucky during the year 2020, as my life wasn't as restricted as many others, but I still had major shifts and changes happening during this year. I therefore wont call this my lockdown story instead I'll call it the story of my personal awakening.

In March 2020, when everything was still normal on this planet, I was at the indigenous festival called Tribal Gathering in Panama. We were totally in our own bubble, celebrating ancient wisdom and our mother earth and hadn't really realized how severe this COVID situation was. It was at the very end of the festival when we realized that many of us weren't allowed to travel back to our home countries. Mexico, where I am from, still allowed people to return, so I did so - immediately. Many of my friends from the festival on the other hand got stuck in Panama for several months and had a very rough time.

I am a traveller and have been for the past 8 years. The thought that I could not travel for some time was a shock especially because I had planned a three-months' Europe tour with indigenous people from the Brazilian Amazon to share their wisdom and ancient medicines. I didn't allow that to take me down a negative spiral and instead I took it as a sign for me to do some work here in my home country and do some travels nationally.

As I returned to Mexico I had already the indigenous shaman waiting for me at my house in Mexico City. So we worked for a month doing several healing ceremonies, which was a beautiful experience and so much needed, especially during this time. While we were doing such meaningful work we also noticed, on a collective level, how the fear was taking over the people's being. We could literally feel the fear vibrationally and how it was taking over. Given that the situation got worse, the indigenous shaman wanted to leave and go back to his tribe in Brazil. But he then couldn't go because his flight got cancelled until further notice. Of course this was heavy on him as he wanted to go back to take care of his family and community.

Luckily as that door closed many others opened and we were able to see how he was meant to stay longer. We were able to continue our work and many new important projects arose. Thanks to that he was able to make an essential amount of money which his community strongly needed. They were suffering severely with the lockdown restrictions and had barely any food. In the whole Amazonian tribal communities he was the only one that was out of the country and able to do work and make money for everyone there.

After he left in May I took off to spend some time in nature. I went east to Veracruz where I stayed for 3 months. I was only able to do this because the world was pretty much in lockdown and there wasn't anything else I could do. I took this opportunity to take time off to work intensely on myself. My focus was to integrate my feminine energy through the embodiment of compassion and love. I did a lot of healing work on myself and my past relationships with the woman I shared a past with. It was a time I needed to take for myself. I encountered so much growth and liberation from this process. I felt inspired, relaxed and evolved as my human avatar.

But as I returned back to the City, I found myself going through some very heavy energetical changes. Out of nowhere I was drained, felt heavy, tired. Not like the usual me. It wasn't just on a physical level. It was also spiritual. This manifested in having to vomit, having vertigo, strong headaches, anxiety and insomnia. I wasn't able to really operate and I stayed at home most of the time. As a traveller, that was new. It was intense and it went on for weeks and weeks. But also during that time I started to receive massive downloads on personal topics as well as collectively and universal. All of a sudden it all made sense. I know this sounds cliché, but that's the only way it can be described. During that time I didn't know what was happening, I just knew something changed in me. In my perception and my whole being. Now looking back I can understand that this was an awakening of some sort.

That's when two new projects came about that I was fully engaged in. One of them is an App that I invented and it finally was coming to birth. Suddenly it all started to flow easily and in a blink of an eye I had a team around me. A team of developers, marketing specialists and other professionals all of a sudden worked for me. My idea wasn't any longer just an idea in my head, it was actually coming to life. That was very exciting and I almost couldn't believe that it was really happening.

In November two indigenous shamans from Brazil came surprisingly back to Mexico. It was surprising because of the whole lockdown situation, we really didn't think that they could come back again, but because of their great effort, it all worked out and they arrived. They came to share their wisdom and medicines for a big project called: Careyes.

I packed my stuff and drove 12 hours up north to Careyes, located on the pacific coast of Mexico. We had planned a one month retreat there with the community that lives there. Careyes, I more than anything have known as a vacation home community, but because of the Pandemic most of the vacation home owners were there. They all decided to leave their cities and stay several months in Careyes. For us this was a great opportunity to share our work and bring healing and transformation into these people's lives. And also to get a lot of funds for the indigenous tribe back in Brazil, who still were desperately in need of help.

For me too this was a great opportunity to fully step into my gifts as a healer and bring to light who I truly am and to share the work I do.

It was an intense time. It was intense as far as teamwork goes. We had many challenges with our team from which I was able to learn a lot from. Only thanks to the experience I went through a couple months earlier, I was able to see it that way. To transmute that energy and learn form it.

Also, this whole experience in Careyes lead me to meet this woman who was (on a 3D level), coincidently, also there in Careyes and participated in our workshops and ceremonies. It was quickly clear for me that the reason I was there was not just because of my personal role, but more to meet her. All I learned during this year was unified with her and I was able to work through all that with her. After only 10 days of meeting her she had to leave back to Los Angeles. We both knew that sooner or later we would see each other again. As she left I noticed that the project there wasn't the same and I decided to go after her. So I took a leap of faith and I hopped on the next flight to Los Angeles - a place I was never drawn to but there I was. And there we were, exploring our beings, diving into new territories and growing. She then came to Mexico and here we still are, working on ourselves and on common projects.

Looking back the year 2020 was the death and re-birth of a cycle. I feel that was not only on an individual level but also collectively. This lead to the detachment of parts within me that were no longer needed to continue my path and the tuning in to a higher vibrational version of myself.

JACKIE, 51, UK CITIZEN RESIDING IN THE ITALIAN ALPS.

Edging our way through the bustling streets of Bangkok, it was hard to see what the future of Covid-19 would look like. Masks are standard practice in many polluted Asian cities, so things didn't look that different to start with. But then masks became obligatory indoors and hand-washing facilities popped up everywhere. We always wore masks and washed our hands a lot when passing through big cities like this, so it still didn't feel that different.

We never much-liked crowded shopping centres anyway. It was late January 2020, and we were on our way home from a two month trip around SE Asia. I worked as a chef and food writer. My partner was a former architectural designer, and we have grown-up twins who were out forging their own paths. We were now on a quest to build a wellness retreat for people to escape to, hidden in the Ligurian Alps. We returned from our trip with heads brimming with ideas for what we could do. The possibilities seemed endlessly exciting!

This hadn't just been a research trip though. The previous year had already taken its toll on my family as we all watched helplessly from the side-lines as my father was battling stage 4 cancer. He was as fierce as they came and encouraged us to go. We had needed this trip in so many ways.

Arriving back in the UK in February, we were suddenly confronted with the situation in Italy, where we are resident - and the apparent gap between what was happening in Asia, compared to Europe. No masks. No guidelines or policy. It was an Italian problem. Until suddenly it wasn't. When Lockdown One hit the UK, we were about to drive back to our new home in Italy, to start building our dream retreat. A place where people could come to heal themselves, to breathe deeply and simply a space to be immersed in nature. Instead we found ourselves staying in our daughter's spare room, whilst she lost her new job, that she had spent a year trying to find. During that first month, we felt pretty lucky. We were together as a family and we had more sunshine than we thought possible for springtime in northern England. But what middle-aged parents want to house share with their grown-up kids for months on end? Or vice versa come to that.

Meanwhile dad was getting sicker. He lived nearby us in Italy, as he had retired to the Riviera many years earlier. He was the main reason we had chosen to be in neighbouring Liguria. For the next month, we focussed all our time on getting home - What paperwork would we need? Did we need our Italian identity cards or just certificate of residency? How could we do the journey safely, both for us and others? By the end of May we finally got there. And suddenly lockdown didn't feel quite so… lockdown-y!

Living an isolated life in the mountains doesn't differ hugely during these challenging Covid-times. Once we got our head around all the form filling and rule exceptions (to visit dad), we found ourselves enjoying what felt like a relatively normal summer. If you can call the summer you are losing your father normal.

We spent as much time as we could visiting Dad, as he was able to continue palliative care at home. If he had gone into hospital, I know I'd be telling a very different story now. Even during the worst of times, to be surrounded by the kind of wondrous beauty that has inspired generations of poets and artists, we knew how fortunate we were to be together. To hold his hand and say the words we needed to share. We felt blessed. As Dad faded, Covid-19 got stronger. Then we faced one of the biggest challenges, to honour his final wishes and bury him alongside his mother back home in Ireland. Somehow we did it. In hindsight, I think this would have been equally traumatic with or without the pandemic.

The impact of the pandemic has delayed our endeavours in Italy without a doubt. But it also gave me the time to be with my family at a time when we needed each other the most. We always thought it would take a few years to build the dream, but now It's starting to stretch us, both in time and money. It can be scary to look too far ahead, and we try to focus on the here and now, creating and developing the elements we can. The slowed down process has allowed us to evolve ideas into realistic plans, which can only be a good thing. I think about what might have been – if we hadn't been brave enough to quit our jobs and come here when we did. If we had decided to wait a few more years, another decade even…

The pandemic has trapped many us where we're at - but if where you're at is an isolated spacious landscape, it's impossible not to feel very lucky! After spending the first two months of lockdown in a city suburb spare room, and listening to neighbouring young mothers trying to entertain several under 5s in a tiny backyard - I was well aware of how differently I even breathed here in Italy. I talked about this to dad, how blessed I feel to be here at this critical point in time, to have space, clean air and mountain streams to swim in. He said, "it's not luck. It's the result of the brave choices you made and realising sooner that there was a better way for you to live". This coming from the man I always thought I disappointed, and who saw me as the mostly flaky one.

It was cancer not the pandemic that made dad reflect on some of his decisions. Wishing he retired earlier. Wishing he had made more time for his family and to just live more of his life. Realising that material wealth means little in the end. I got to see the joy he felt at seeing us move here and start to build the dream. No doubt he led me to this place but we're now finding our own way to be here. It's going to continue to be a slow process of growth – for the retreat project and for us, learning to make a life and living in this landscape. And I do feel lucky (sorry dad). I just know it takes both. Brave decisions have to come first though. I learnt that from my father.

SIMON, 38, UK CITIZEN TEACHING IN JAPAN.

As Covid-19 cases started to skyrocket in various parts of the world, especially my native British Isles, I took to wearing masks at work here in Japan, where I've been working as an English teacher.

It's not unusual to wear a mask in public here, but teachers tend to only wear them when they're sick. One of my co-teachers seemed to supress a smile when he enquired about my new look after I told him it was pandemic-related. It wasn't being taken as seriously here as it was abroad. On the following Monday, however, all teachers had to comply with 'ninja chic'.

The response by the Japanese government was slow. The reported numbers of cases were low in comparison to corona hot spots. A fellow foreign teacher in a Facebook support group told of the extreme difficulty and diversions she'd been through just trying to get a Covid test - despite displaying the symptoms. Were the rumours true? Was the government under-reporting cases so they could keep the Olympics on track, so to speak?

It seemed to take an age for Japan to finally postpone their prestige event.

The cancellation of the 2020 Tokyo Olympics was swiftly followed by a declaration of a state of emergency. Unlike the rest of the world, where governments had enforced prison-style 'lockdowns', here in Japan we were given more of a strong suggestion to stay home and avoid big crowds.

For the first month of this invisible lockdown, I clocked in to a school with no students. It was a dizzying sensation as I sat in the middle of a busy room of 40 Japanese teachers, all somehow hurrying about their daily grind, despite there being nobody to teach. The Japanese work environment isn't known for its relaxed approach.

Based in Yokohama, I kept my distance from Tokyo for about three weeks, until I ventured into the capital to visit my girlfriend again. The reported cases of just over 100 infections a day seemed low enough to risk it. Erico lived off seemingly one of the busiest pedestrian stretches in Japan, Takeshita Street in the bubble-gum pop fashion district of Harajuku.

Typically packed with a slow-moving mix of rainbow-coloured youth and international tourists, the atmosphere was now more like one of Tokyo's more non-descript alleys. The central Yamanote train line, usually bustling on a Saturday, mirrored Takeshita's atypical emptiness. Tokyo as a whole felt like it had opened up its most popular areas for a private viewing.

As Japanese citizens seemed to casually sail into the choppy corona seas with a sense of calm, I watched on through the black mirror of social media at my fellow Brits, with a mixture of disappointment and amusement.

Shoppers in England argued with each other about social distancing whilst spaced out in long lines in supermarket car parks. Police scolded picnickers in parks. Cyclists barked at pedestrians to stay the full two metres clear of them on country lanes. Friends made outrageous Facebook statuses - that others had disobeyed the government and visited such controversial spots as national park mountains and waterfalls. A drone followed a dog walker in the Peak District. A drone walked a dog in Cypress. And who could forget the Americans, overloading their trolleys with that most precious of resources, toilet roll, and duelling it out in the aisles for the final pack of 24.

Whilst you might find the rice shelves in Japanese supermarkets depleted the day before a typhoon is forecast, the rest of the shelves are still decently stocked. After seeing images of ransacked shelves in Tesco, Sainsbury's and other British supermarkets, it was almost a guilty sensation strolling through the bountiful food forest of my local supplier, a supersized 7-11. Yet there was also a relief that I was reaping some benefits from the gamble to move to Japan, which hadn't paid off so much in 2019. We were still living a relatively normal life here.

As breadline workers around the world found themselves without a plan B, I appreciated the fact that the company I work for was large enough to hold on to their staff. The various company branches take a very generous helping from the financial pot provided by the Japanese government, the rations handed onto us leading to a high turnover. Had I been working for a smaller businesses or an independent school, it could have been a different story.

After six weeks under a state of emergency, the students came back to school. There was a fresh batch of over two hundred 12-13 year olds, starting their first year of junior high school a little later than usual. It was great to have 600 plus kids and the energy they brought back onto the premises, even if their faces were only partially visible. I was able to wear a plastic mouth guard for teaching so students could trace my mouth movements for those tricky English sounds.

As a communication teacher, the lessons were restricted at first in terms of the types of activities we could do. Yet in break times the students would be clambering all over each other, hugging, wrestling, giving piggy backs and all the usual kids' stuff. The class restrictions seemed a little academic, so it was a relief for everyone when we got back to group activities more quickly than the government would care to know about. This wasn't just for practical purposes, but also just for the kids to feel human again.

With domestic travel the only option, my girlfriend and I took a short summer trip to the spectacular Kansai region of central Japan, visiting Osaka, Nara and Kyoto.

Before arriving at the hotel, we hopped off the train at my favourite neighbourhood in Osaka, the retro-cool Shinsekei.

Two things struck us here.

Firstly, the lack of locals and tourists alike had sucked the place dry of its typically vibrant atmosphere. More staff stood outside restaurant entrances than there were pedestrians. We decided lunch would be Takoyaki - deep-fried octopus, one of Osaka's specialities.

The second thing that struck us was the intense heat, which had us bed-bound for the rest of the day. The Japanese summer takes no prisoner: future Olympians take note.

In the cool of the evening we went back to Shinsekei, to a restaurant specializing in another of Osaka's specialities: the pancake-like okonomiyaki. Walking back to the hotel, the usually buzzing neon-lit shopping district of Shinsaibashi was almost completely shut down by 9pm, a curious sight for a Saturday night.

We took a daytrip to Nara, Japan's first capital, the next day. Unlike Osaka, the atmosphere in this enchanting UNESCO-protected time capsule benefitted from the lack of tourists, at least from our selfish desires. Nara, interwoven with Shinto and Buddhist temples, traditional houses and thousands of free-roaming sika deer, is gorgeous. Riding electric bicycles around the place felt like we'd travelled far further than the casual 40 minutes it took from Osaka; no big crowds meant far less foot traffic to avoid.

The last location on our brief getaway was Japan's second ancient capital, Kyoto. Many small businesses were closed and we soon discovered that we had entered a period known as 'Obon', where many people leave town to visit relatives. Add to that the blisteringly hot temps of Kyoto's basin landscape with no international tourists coming through, and this was a very different Kyoto experience to past visits.

Like the tourist-reliant businesses of Shinsekai, there was an air of desperation whenever we stepped foot in a souvenir shop. Whilst I was sympathetic to their plight, and we circulated as much yen as we could, I was also aware of this rare period of time, exploring the famous city, as one of the few foreign faces.

Kyoto felt more like an off the beaten track hidden gem. That said, it also felt like an oven.

Fast forward a year and I've still yet to see most of the first graders' faces. In fact, it was only recently when I saw the unmasked face of a new co-teacher I've shared a classroom with for about a year.

Many of the stresses people suffered from in 2020, the sense of social isolation and separation from loved ones, I'd been through the year before by proxy of being an immigrant. The poor living conditions dealt by my company added to some low times. However, a lot of that dust settled heading into 2020, in stark contrast to countless others whose problems were just about to start.

Now, as I write this in early 2021, my time in Japan is coming to an end. I hope to be with friends and family in about a month. Britain seems to be nearing the end of its third, and hopefully final, lockdown. Yet with daily reports of virus variants, everything is still very much up in the air. There's a joke about flights here somewhere.

This was my account from what many think of as a strange country. I get the feeling that the UK I'll be returning to will feel a lot stranger than Japan after the year that was.

BECCA, 32 UK CITIZEN LIVING IN BASQUE REGION, SPAIN.

March 2020. Camping with friends and enjoying.

We had planned to stay in the south of France for a few more weeks in search of a new home for me and my tiny family, Me, my partner and my cheeky 2 year old son. Always on the hunt for the perfect place, to plant ourselves and grow roots. Our nomadic days left us eager to find our own place.

The local market was lively and colourful as always - I started to overhear people chattering about some virus and borders closing. I didn't really think much of it. I guess I expected it to be another poor country far away from ours. My disconnection from our privileged life to the rest of the world. We always think we are untouchable; these things happen to other people, not to us. It soon caught up to me that it was closer to home when the rumours spread and people started to panic - that the markets were closing, businesses had to close. This virus was spreading fast.

News exploded, Once I heard the borders were closing, I searched frantically for information. Our current home lies on the border of Spain and France in the Basque region, lost in the hills, an off grid experiment, a renovated barn, sometimes not enough sun. We were taking care of it for an old hippy, who fancied a sunnier life in the Canaries. A bit rough around the edges but it was our home for the past year, our safe haven.

We drove back as soon as we could. The whole drive I was excited and a bit scared, is this it? humanity's end - over a virus? Something the Sci-Fi movies made blockbusters over numerous times and gave me a fantastic graphic visual of how it was all going to play out. First the headlines I discovered were mostly of people hoarding bog rolls, this cracked me up. Surely in a crisis people can wash their arses with water? Maybe my travelling days didn't leave me much room for compassion regarding the paper looters. I became angry that people were just out for themselves. But what? how serious is it?

We made it home, a bubble from the chaos, I was so appreciative we had this place, all the times I complained and actually we were pretty set up for the zombie apocalypse, I was filled with fear and total excitement, buzzing from the unknown, are we prepared?

Rice.... check. High ground... check. Pitch forks... check. Cool... now what?

Honestly the coming days was spent scrolling the first news of lockdown. It was wild - conspiracies and theories coming from every angle, some totally outrageous. We were told to stay in our homes and only leave for necessities. The first few days were really dark and scary for me, I felt safe in my house, but what the hell was going on out there?!

I couldn't help thinking how so inevitable it was that something like this was upon us? A virus, literally the entire world stopped, STOPPED. Humanity and all its technological intelligence, our lives we take for granted! It was a unnerving but humbling moment that no matter what we did as a race, nothing can stop the force of nature.

I sat at home feeling anxious, I was frightened for my parents, I suddenly felt so far away from them now, if something happened I couldn't get to them. My mind became encumbered with information, convinced the world, as we know it, was ending.

My persistent need to decipher the truth, what the hell was going on? I became totally sucked into a wormhole of theory and conspiracy on the social platform. Absolute bombardment of information. It seemed everyone was doing the same as me, scrambling to know what the truth is, how this virus came about? How serious is it? I was swinging between believing the world is run by vampires - creating a virus to implement total control and feed off our fear, to the even scarier prospect that nobody is in control or has a clue how to save us. Both these thought processes equally terrifying, and pushed me into temporary madness . Ermmmmm, let's take a break from the screen a bit, shall we hey?

The separation of people became more apparent. One side believing it's all totally orchestrated, refusing to wear masks. The others, lost in fear and severity of the virus, people slinging statistics and information to one another on the social platform, trying to prove their point.

The internet, a web of connection, became a cancer of misinterpreted information, left and right wing ideas on one platform. The luxury of having so much time on our hands to explore and research a wormhole of infinite theory and possibility, it's just mad! I had to stop. The same web of connection over the coming months became the main source to maintain community, speak to family, support and share knowledge, people posting fun ridiculous home-made videos, documenting lockdown delirium. Priceless laugher.

Over the coming weeks my initial thought that community will be destroyed thanks to the bog roll robbers, quickly turned to heart explosive trust in humanity. Actually for the first time we were a GLOBAL community, all experiencing and talking about the same thing, this comforted me.

Stories of people helping and caring for each other where they could, tales of people singing from their balconies to serenade their lonely neighbours. People cheering on the streets in the evening time to support the NHS and all their hard work. All these tiny victories of communities coming together in times of hardship, people finding what they could do to spread a bit of love. Such duality in this whole experience, people stripped back to just themselves, time to stop. In a world of constant distraction and entertainment it was a respite for a lot of us.

After the small internet surfing obsession, I decided to set up my hardcore exercise regime, 2 mornings in - it was easily forgotten... But I promised to stay away from the social media circus and just be.

Actually this was the first time in my life I wasn't chasing anything, I accepted I had nowhere to go, nobody to see. I wasn't missing out on anything, this gave me immense comfort and a 'thank fuck for that' feeling. It was epic. For the first time in my life just totally embracing that I was exactly where I needed to be. The valley where my home lies gave me so much nurturing and love - the nature just blows my mind. Total gratitude - we had this entire place to play in and create a bubble with not a person or mask in sight for miles.

I went deep into my psyche, so much time without distraction exploring and meeting myself really for the first time in 32 years, this 'person' I had always ran away from and spent my life avoiding. Those first few months were a rollercoaster of despair, sorrow, joy and acceptance, I'm knee deep in that journey still. The lockdown kickstarted this vortex of self-exploration that I would have circumvented a lot longer.
The valley nurtured us - spring was a good time to learn how to forage - stories of food shortages looming. We studied textbooks of local flowers and natural remedies - leaves, bark and buds, making flower salads, wild leaf pesto, daisy creams and nettle face masks. Invaluable knowledge! My son learnt the tricks of nature - these moments just reinforced our connection to the little things and how this way of life, amongst its hard moments, was so true and meant so much to us.

We kept shopping trips to every ten days, not out of fear of Covid, but from just the heaviness of it all. We had to sign papers to declare what and why we were leaving our home - border control checking all our movements to move into France - too much to do... to be able to go shopping. The supermarkets became some weird meeting of faceless characters, everyone with a mask, standing separate and distant in lines, nobody talking to each other, it was so heavy - disinfectant everywhere, be clean, clean, clean! I was becoming paranoid my little boy would get scared of bacteria and contact with people. I was always conscious of people watching me if I bought too much rice or the extra bottle of olive oil in the first few weeks. The litter of surgical masks eerily floating in the countryside as rubbish!

Living on the border means people come to buy boxes of cheap tobacco, when there is a sanitary lung virus threatening us all, why not hey! Helicopters flying over the beach to check nobody was enjoying the sand too much, you had to keep walking, in clockwise motion, patrollers checking the beach if you fancied a cheeky sit down far away from anyone else. One woman jumped across the road and nearly fell over when she saw me coming, it was all getting a bit silly. Rules coming out of nowhere and contradicting themselves, it was all so confusing.

Luckily we can walk for miles and miles over the hills, nobody around, wild horses parade our area so every now and again I would find a skeleton and take it home as a trophy, I decided to paint the skull, it was pretty impressive, so much time and moments of clarity gone into create this piece - I sold it straight away, so content I could have a little income in a time where no jobs were available to us - a weird and odd venture but it still supports us to this day, I find such joy in this odd little craft I discovered roaming the hills. Even 800 metres high I sometimes find a lonely old farmer with his mask on looking at the mountains, the fear even from fresh air.

The elderly, so much more risk for them, a year later and my grandma and her husband, who both had heart and lung problems, haven't left their house, waiting for the day the vaccine comes and they can see family, talk to the neighbour without fear, hug their grandchildren. These times have been especially hard for them, the television for company, but at least they have each other, so many elderly were alone during these times. Loneliness is the biggest sadness through all of this. I can only imagine the mental health issues people have had to face during these times, through fear of losing their jobs, having nobody to visit them ,being alone with their thoughts. It's not an easy process. We had a positive experience during these months, and for that I'm grateful. So many people have their own stories that weren't as positive at all.

After the initial three months they started to lift the regulations. June came and everyone was allowed to play a little bit, restaurants slowly opened, a lot had closed down, the government had managed to help small business a little to keep them running, but this wasn't the case for all of them. This still continues, the economy has taken an upheaval, only the future will see how we make it through and pick ourselves up.

A year later masks are still obliged to be worn, it's become the norm, sometimes I still forget to take one with me and have to tie an old scarf around my mouth in the hope I don't get told off by somebody. I still find myself holding my breath under the masks.

Young kids in school are obliged to wear masks here in Spain. My 2 year old went to the park after school hours to play with the other children, they ran from him like he is a little alien, wondering why this peculiar creature didn't have his face covered - he asked me for a little mask so he didn't feel left out. The mask wearing is the hardest for me to see on the little ones - people say they will get used to it, but that's exactly what I'm afraid of.

A year later and vaccines have started to be given, signs of hope of having our freedom back and spring coming again. People are a lot more cheery and excited! The sunshine will make it harder for people to follow the lockdown laws, people are rearing to get out and start living again. The elbow tap has become the new thing to do here instead of the typical 2 kiss on the cheek French-style. I look forward to the days I don't need permission to give somebody a big cuddle!!

I think the world is in anticipation for the next chapter.

For the moment we are still in our home in the valley, a year ago I wanted to run away and find something more exciting, and lively. Our luxury freedom to move meant we had the whole world to explore, this luxury actually had me feeling really lost. Honestly the place I wanted to leave and run from has nurtured, watered, healed and gift-ed me and my family in the wildest strangest most evolutionary time of our lives. In this little converted sheep shed, I feel stronger and more trusting than ever.

I still have no answers, or know what the hell is going on.
But I accept it, life is curious and odd and so surprising in a myriad of ways.

It has strengthened us all in one way or another.
No matter what experience we had we will never forget this.

Such a poignant time in our lives when the world just stopped.
Let's see what the future brings us all.....

Personally… I can't wait for a big crowded dancefloor.

CATARINA, 35 PORTUGAL.

On the 22nd of January 2020 exactly at 8.43am, from the East, Aquarius was rising. Aligned with the same constellation, was the Sun of that day. At that precise moment, with the help of my partner, I gave birth to our first son.
In his first days in this world, we were floating in a cocktail of oxytocin and serotonin, experiencing the most profound and absolute Love of our lives. On a very distant layer of reality we could listen to a continuous noise. Coming and going, the fuss about something that was happening in China felt constant, yet far away. And so, it was easy to ignore. From our bubble, in Lisbon, we were testifying the miracle of life: Rodrigo was finally here and nothing else mattered.
My name is Catarina and on that day I was born as a mother, at the same time that the maiden I once was died forever. Since then I've been shedding my old skin, slowly uncovering my mature colours in this new cycle of my existence. It was fated that the year of the big

transition of my life as a woman would coincide with one of the most challenging years of our generation.

Two months after our birth, we moved to the UK. As Chris, my partner is a British citizen, we had decided to live in Canterbury, Kent, for around five years and then return to Portugal, to get some land and live as autonomous and self-sustainable as possible. We believed that we had to make real money to get us there and it was that belief that brought us to the UK – right in the first peak of the Covid-19 pandemic.

At this moment the noise was not distant anymore, it was fully here. And there too, it was just everywhere. Shortly after our arrival the full lockdown was declared and so we remained in the same bubble, just in a new country.

In those confinement days, we lived the darkest hours of this planetary shift. Nothing was certain, no one knew what was about to happen, it felt like we were on the verge of an apocalyptic future.

And so, from the inside of our house, from inside of ourselves, a seedling started to emerge. Finding its way to reach daylight, the vision became clearer. Feeding itself in the fertile ground of hardship, it became stronger and made us take a profound look at our priorities in life: space, freedom, connectedness with Mother Earth, healthy food, community and bonfires.

The new enclosed, confined, hermetic and tech-dependent reality that this virus was proposing, looked to us too permanent and we decided we wouldn't wait for it to pass, cause the truth is: none of us knows if it will pass and, if it does, what will follow.

So, even if we loved the place where we had just arrived (yes, I am still madly in love with Canterbury), we decided to follow the voice inside. Our intuition was urging us to live our dream in our present and to provide our son with freedom in these uncertain years of mankind's evolution. From the locked reality of our little house we decided that our family wouldn't grow inside the boundaries of the city, but instead we would have the horizon as a companion, daily kissing the earth with our feet. Rodrigo would learn to care for the water, the soil and the fire, his golden locks kissed by the gentle winds of never ending planes and mounts.

In August of 2020, only 5 months after arriving in the UK, we decided to return to Portugal and establish ourselves in Alentejo, the remote interior in the country's south. That's where we are now - in my ancestors' land - learning to grow food, while finding sustainable ways to conserve water and regenerate soil. Here, away from the hustle and bustle, we are building our house and life project.

This decision would, probably, have taken us many years more if it wasn't for the 'special' circumstances of last year. They pushed us beyond our fear, made us notice the impermanent fragility of life and encouraged us to new and, maybe, uninviting territories. What we do with the time that is given to us is our own responsibility. This is our way.

I pray for all that give their lives and energy to the battle of our time. May you be blessed and protected.

With love,

Catarina Costa e Palma, 6 of March 2021, Alentejo

LEE, 29 AUSTRALIAN CITIZEN IN BERLIN

The year 2020. Where does one begin? What a rollercoaster of emotions for all of us! In my wildest dreams I could not have imagined this happening within my lifetime, but yet it did. This pandemic came straight out of the left field for me and I am here to share my story with you.

The end of 2019 was fantastic. I had arrived in Europe from Australia in June and my long-awaited adventure had begun. Ten years I had waited to land on the magical earth of Europe; ten years I had waited to travel the world and lead a life of adventure. I had finally found my career path and purpose in life and serendipity was leading me there. Settling in Berlin was not my plan, visiting Germany this early on in my trip was not at all in my vision, but yet Berlin is where I found myself and wow, did I fall in love. I fell in love with the air, the people, the openness and honesty, the fashion, the art and all its energy. My savings were standing tall and I felt secure and prosperous, preparing 2020 and 2021 carefully and purposefully. I had never been so excited about my future. My plan was organised…

- March, I was in Vienna to study for two weeks then I planned to travel around.(I made it to Vienna for my study, but my trip was cut short)
- April, I was back in Berlin to begin my long-awaited tattoo.
- May, I was to be in the beautiful coast of Spain, the breathtaking Costa Brava for two weeks studying 'Bodywork and Trauma healing'.
- June my friend Lisa and I were to drive down the coast of Spain.
- July and August are Festival time, time to work and play.
- September is back to Berlin for another tattoo session and Birthday celebrations.
- October is adventure time to Jakarta and then flying to Bali to meet my family and partner whom I had not seen in over 12 months.
- Mid November, I would surprise my family by flying back with them to Australia for Christmas and New Years.
- January 2021, my partner and I vacationing in an undecided location while she is on holidays from work.

- February 2021, back to Europe to finish off my last pieces of study over the next 4 months.
- May 2021, heading over to California to graduate from my study and then travel for 3 months.

What a magnificent journey I was to embark on only for it to come crashing down around me piece by piece. Now begins the hard journey that was 2020, a spiralling gush of wind knocking me into a cold sea of unchartered emotions.

The Corona Virus. Three words that were occasionally circling the globe at the beginning of the year were now becoming a household name. In 2003 SARS broke, Ebola in 2013, both had not spread globally so who would have thought this new virus would take another path. More and more negative stories were heard about the spread and danger, yet my mind pushed away the thought of a global pandemic, complete denial of the possibility. The weeks continued and the spread became worse by the day, from the east to the west, country to country with no end in sight.

In early March, Germany went into full lockdown as I came back from Austria. I am self-employed but contracted and suddenly found myself without work. The apartment I was residing in was dark and gloomy, lifeless as if the sun could not find us. How was I to stay here for an undecided period of time? During the end of 2019 I found myself a new friend, a true kindred spirit who humbly offered her home to me during this uncertain time. My spirits lifted and into isolation we went, her and I both homebodies immensely enjoying the down time together with the sunshine filling the house with warmth. Puzzles, boardgames, music and laughter, day after day, week after week. Wine and stories, books and movies, all seemed quiet and perfect. This lockdown was much needed, a break from work and life, a chance for all of us to slow down and reconnect with ourselves. I also began the year studying Biomedicine online and this seemed to be the perfect opportunity to concentrate on study. When else do we find a clear elongated period of time? This lock down will not last long, a few months and the world will restart fresh and recharged. I was in complete denial of the gravity of the situation. A glass half full was my demeanour, high spirits were all that resided within me, patiently but eagerly waiting for my adventure to come.

The weeks were passing by and no end to the virus in sight. My new tattoo I had been long awaiting now cancelled, my flight to Spain now cancelled, my study now moved forward until August. Yet I found myself still glass half full just rearranging a few things in my plan.

The end of Spring was coming faster now, May seemed to arrive in the blink of the eye and yet no end in sight for the virus. Summer was right around the corner and lockdown requirements began to ease, restaurants and cafes were reopening. The sun settled high in the sky now, the trees were in full bloom and the air was becoming sweet with the taste of the scented flowers covering the streets. The lakes opened and a sea of people looking for a moment of coolness begun to explore the outside world again. Distancing from one another in order to keep the virus at bay seemed to be working. The world it seemed was slowly healing.

I was ready. Ready for my adventure, ready for August to come and for the Spanish air to fill my lungs. Denial still filled my essence and hope still lingered. I had studied hard and passed my first exam with high marks in June. There would be no festival dancing this year. June swept through and July came rushing forward. Maybe we should take this time to travel while the borders are open and that's what we did. A two-week trip across Germany, Czechia, Austria, Croatia, Slovenia and Italy. Driving windows down and fresh summer air pouring in, wonder filling our hearts. Beautiful landscapes and forests of green, mesmerising lakes of blue and mountains of gold under the warm summer sun. Travelling during this time was lovely as not many others were. The walks were not overcrowded with tourists nor were the roads. Venice had never been so quiet. It was as if the whole city was created just for us. Truly a trip I will never forget.

The end of July found us home in Berlin and I was excited to head to Spain. Denial seemed to still be seeded deep within my mind, but word arrived shortly after that my study had been cancelled. Slowly I begun to feel less hopeful, I begun to feel heavy and confused.

August found me in a state of disillusion and disbelief. I had a feeling very uncommon to me, a deep growling pain. Easily vexed I had become, contentious to all those in my life, illusive I was beginning to feel. The days were hard to breathe and the nights were suffocating as my heart was slowly sinking. I felt a blazing fire, deep within me, the spread of it completely immersing within my veins. My mind was trying to escape my body, I found myself shaking, deeply trembling under the pressure of my emotions. I had no words to describe my state, for the new feeling inside me, all I could do was let it be. Let it transpire into what it wanted to become. Anger. Anger towards myself and towards the world.

September came and I found myself shifting from red to longing, longing for some resemblance of my plan, was anything going to come to fruition? Praying to Gaia that my trip to Jakarta and Bali was still on the horizon, I knew deep in my heart my pleads would ultimately be unanswered. But I could not stop myself from forming the words on my lips 'please, just one thing'. Berlins restrictions seemed to be lifting a little more each day as did my prospects of work and by the end of September I found myself working again. Happiness and hope begun to fill my cup, my prayers were being answered, thank you Gaia for heeding my invocation but a measly week later back into lock down we went.

How had I thought things would go smoothly from here on out? I hoped but I knew my prayers would ultimately go unanswered. I had got my hopes up and now only snickering and guffaws on a continual loop, filling my ears and plunging me into darkness.

October began with disassociation and complete severance of myself, darkness following me like the shadow of a falconer. Down and down the rabbit hole I was tumbling, happiness had left my idea of life as the darkness of winter began to loom. Should I go home to Australia with my family or should I ride out the virus that had now become my enemy? If I go home to Australia, have I failed in my quest to start a new life? All my life I had wished to escape from the constraints of societal expectations. I wanted to travel and study, explore and wonder. Was going back home to my country a failure? No money left and no work, no idea what I was going to do now, my whole beautiful plan no longer existed yet I could not seem to let it go. My beautiful plan which I had worked so hard for, my beautiful plan which I was ready for, my perfect adventure I had long waited for - now nothing. Nothing but ash left behind from the devastating uncontrollable hell fire that was 2020.

Weeks passed by with no sense of time, days had no meaning and words of comfort lost their sense. Isolation not only in my surroundings but complete lockdown in my mind. I had come to a crossroads now; which direction was I to go in? Which direction was the right one? What if I make a mistake and choose the wrong path? Round and round the questions circled my mind, dizzy from the never-ending carousel. Just wait I would tell myself but wait for what? Life is now, get up and move forward, just move anywhere. Take a step. Just begin. Constant fighting back and forth. Just make a choice, but the darkness was winning and in the middle of the crossroads I stayed.

2021 and into the new year, we had survived 2020 and the virus. Somewhere, somehow in my mind I had convinced myself that 2021 would be a new year that was corona free. Why had I thought this? How had I convinced myself that this pandemic would only last 12 months and magically disappear? A short new year's pep talk by my partner had instantly and suddenly shocked me back into reality and now I look back at my naivety and giggle to myself, I look back at my denial and smile at myself. We enter into 2021 with no ending on the horizon, but I have found myself entering the year with a new sense of self. I have awoken out of the spell that imprisoned me. I can now breathe the fresh air. The dark claws that had pierced my skin had finally let go and acceptance now fills the rabbit hole. During 2020 I had experienced a rainbow of emotions, a whirlpool of what I now know to be grief. I had gone through the five stages of grief unaware that this was my reality.

Denial, Anger, Bargaining, Depression and Acceptance.

I was mourning for my beautiful plan that I had created; I was grieving my adventure and journey that I had long waited for. Now I was slowly letting go of the path I thought was meant to be and slowing coming into the path I am truly meant to be on. Everything happens for a reason and the way it should, Gaia never makes mistakes; these are words I have always lived by but somehow utterly forgotten. I had made a new Berlin friend for a reason, so I did not have to be alone during this time. I had put off studying for years but began and finished my year in Biomedicine at the perfect time to focus. Serendipity was still following me. I have found my path once more and back home to Australia I fly to begin a new adventure. I am leaving 2020 in 2020 and continuing to write my story on the paper life gives me one day at a time. This is the hard but wonderful lesson this pandemic has given me, and I am truly grateful for without the darkness we cannot know the light.

RICHI, 41 SWINDON UK.

March 2020

When the pandemic first hit I thought what the hell is this. It was around my birthday, 18th March and we had planned a weekend in London, bar crawls, food and clubbing at a new music venue. Unfortunately it was all cancelled. We were gutted. We were isolated in our home like prisoners, with no one to see and nothing to do. I found it really weird. No one really knew what they were doing, including our government. The rules were ridiculous and if what they said was true, then they should've acted faster and closed the boarders.

I had to still go to work and have done so ever since. My work was also slow in protecting us with PPE (personal protective equipment) and never had any plan in place. It took them a long while to protect us, but still had us working in 10 different properties a day. Due to the fact that me and my wife Joanna are key-workers as a plumber and a night manager at a care home, I was allowed to have two days off a week to look after our children while they were off school. But my work soon changed their minds after a month and I was back working in a lot of properties. We argued the point that we should only be doing emergency work due to the pandemic. We are still in the same argument in 2021 and there's still no change. We are still entering 10 or more properties a day completing non-essential work. My work just does not care for their Tradesman. We are not allowed in the office because we will put the office staff at risk, but it's ok if we fall ill and give it to our family? Most managers are working from the comfort of their own home so why would they care about us. I feel like I'm worth nothing after showing my dedication for over 26 years.

In April my wife Joanna fell really ill. At the time we were trying for another baby. It was about 1.30am and I kept hearing the house phone, but still half a sleep, so thought nothing of it. It rang again so I rushed down to answer and it wasn't good news at all. Joanna went into cardiac arrest while at work. So I had to wake the kids up and tell them and I also wasn't allowed to go to the hospital due to Covid19. I've never been so scared. So I had to play the waiting game and finally had a call to say she was doing well and that I could pick her up late that morning. Joanna didn't look too good and throughout the day got worse and ended up going into cardiac arrest again, for a second time that same day. So I had to call the hospital to pick her up, while I had to keep the children upstairs. It was horrible to see. While in hospital they gave a treatment to thin the blood which helped a lot. They said it was a side effect of the contraceptive pill and caused a blood clot because Joanna was on it for so long. So please girls be very careful with medication you are given. And at the same time we found out Joanna was pregnant with twins, so we were over the moon. After a week Joanna went back to hospital for a check up and unfortunately the babies had stopped growing, but we had to wait another two weeks for another checkup, it was the longest two weeks of our lives. We had extremely sad news, we lost our beautiful twins. Joanna had to have them removed straight away and without being put to sleep due to Covid 19. Joanna had to go through all this on her own due to me not being allowed in the hospital.

But we came together as a family and are stronger than ever. This pandemic has changed us as a family, made us realise what we have and how much we love and need each other. And we are now strong for our children, appreciating family time together. Now all is not lost. We have some exciting news - we are expecting a little boy, due 2nd June 2021. Joanna is well, the family is well and the baby is doing amazingly well too. And we are super excited to meet this little dude. After everything we've been through, we have a little miracle. But, not forgetting the beautiful twins, of course we are thinking of them all the time and we will light two candles on the 7th May each year to remember them.

NANN, 27 THAILAND.

Lock down diary from Koh Phangan, Thailand

2020 is gonna be my year. At least that is what I thought at the beginning of the year; promotion, travel plans, new career opportunities and love life. Don't they say God laughs when you make plans, comes April, I lost my job, got my heart broken and there goes my travel.

I'm a Traditional Chinese Medicine doctor and acupuncturist, live and work in the beautiful island of Thailand "Koh Phangan" If you have been here, you know of its magic. If you haven't been here… hope one day you feel the call to come.

The Sanctuary Thailand, I don't think there is a better place to be locked down in. A famous wellness destination. Remotely tucked away from the rest of the world, beautiful ocean to swim, sunshine, tropical fruits. Decision making by the beginning of lock down is difficult, as there are many people choosing to go home to their loved ones or whatever way to face the uncertainty. I, however, was not in the position of making any decisions. It came down to the only option available. Stay put, I've worked here for the last 2 years. As much as I love to call it home, it was not quite. However, my previous boss invited me to stay. For someone who has to look out for myself most of the time, that kindness is everything.

May

Weeks after the lockdown, I can't be any more happier. Waking up to sunrise every day and the feeling of no rush to be anywhere. It's my favourite month of the year, my birthday. Since I won't be traveling anywhere there is no wrong of spoiling myself a little bit. All 5 star hotels and villas are at a great discount. I don't see why not.

June

People. I don't think I've been around many people anymore. All of the sudden, there're many people moved into the beach. Gatherings, dinners and beach parties. I'm not quite sure how I feel being around this many people now, It might take some time for me to feel normal around people again. But sure I don't mind these parties... However, all parties have to come to an end. When my best friend here decided to take on her journey elsewhere. I feel the sudden shift in me. Europe is now open for Summer. I'm happy that she is ready for her new adventure. And so I am, we share so much good time, but by that point we both want to be somewhere else. Once in a while, there are some dark days and nights. Some dark thoughts come by, so scary I can't tell anyone. At one point the thought of self sabotage happens, just like in an old movie film. I saw a vision, what showed to me was all the lives I lived, one after another, I gave up, and abandoned myself...What would be the lessons? That day, many friends either show up at my place or call me, quite unusual. I'll take that as a sign.

July

When there are people there are conflicts. A small miscommunication leads to harsh words and difficult situations. As much as I don't want to be involved, these people are my friends and neighbours. By this time all I want is to move on and start over. No point of me being here anymore. I booked my flight, maybe my hometown or a new city. Movement would help me see better.

August

As soon as I get on the truck to leave Sanctuary, trees fall down in front of the car. Not once but twice, the driver said don't go, they don't want you to leave. What he meant was the protector of the land, the high spirit. I usually call her Mama, and she is not pleased with my decision. So said him. But I have made my mind.

At farewell dinner, my friend phones an old friend of hers in the US. "She's a psychic, ask her about your decision" After the tree story, none of my friends think it's a good idea for me to leave. As I took that call, I got the biggest chills all over. "Don't get on that plane," she said. "It will be the end of you, within 3 months from now on you will get into an accident, deadly. Your protector wants you here, and she will make sure you are where she wants you to. Now or later don't fight it".

But let's be honest here, since when I listen to what people say. That night the storm hit the island, the biggest wave we ever have in the past few months. I decided to wait out just a few more days, I still can catch my flight. A day before my flight, one of the ferries sank down the ocean with 20 people missing. Suddenly, there are no more ferries running. Here my only ride out. Worst of all I got into a motorbike accident, stitches and cost of treatments. And it leaves my phone as a goner. I'm now stuck on the island! Again!

I packed 7 boxes and sent them to be stored somewhere. "If I can get my stuff back I will stay here" or at least that is what I thought to myself. And guess what, after 3 days since I left Sanctuary, I managed to take back a box from the shipment. I found myself a new house, new mobile, new ride despite all the trouble I still need to be in Bangkok in a few weeks time and that I have made my mind.

In the process of transitions. I got Dengue. What on earth, I have lived in tropical places all my life. Now I got dengue from the least expected place ever! You thought you know pain, well not until Dengue... How helpless you feel, no strength, no appetite, just pain all over your body. Every vertebrae of my spinal, my skull and joint. It felt like I was run over by a car. I can barely open a bottle of water myself. My inner ear was infected and I lost my balance. Here I am in a new house, nobody knows where I live, nobody knows how I am doing. All by myself feeling all weak, useless, all alone.

By day 9, one of the girls reached out to me. We haven't been in contact for a while. The lesson is to know that it is ok to ask for help. The next thing you know, a friend who you thought you lost touch gets on the bike in the dark, to bring you water, fruits and medicine. Oh how superficial I appreciate my relationships with people. How I never truly know love or recognize one. How easy it is for me to run away from it. Not only I recovered from the Dengue, I recovered from all of my heart broken, I recovered from the virus that ran deep in my belief and I recovered from the fear of love.

I went back to Sanctuary after that. To make amends with my fear and what I am running away from.

September

I haven't been truly honest to myself. I'm in love. One of the reasons I left Sanctuary was my broken heart, once again. I can never be with the man I love or I thought I can never be with him. Here I am, confronting, all the words I wish I share and the feeling I've been dismissing. Put all my cards on the table, no ego, no regret, no expectation, I am ready to walk away from this. And once again, I left the Sanctuary, but this time I know I'll come back.

October

If there's such a thing as new life, new light. I'm now experiencing it. An old friend of mine reached out, she's opening a new healing centre and she thinks I'm a good fit to the team. A couple weeks ago, I feel like I was done with this place and there was nothing left for me. Here on the first meeting, I feel like I meant to meet all of these people, whether I will work in the project or not, we meant to cross paths. Stories are told, word to word. We're not facing this difficulty alone. I'm on my journey, as are many people. Once again, I deeply appreciate this island.

November

The man I love.. Just like any story, romance needs to be mentioned. A few months earlier, my story can't be told to anyone. I was having an affair. Not like I was sleeping with the guy or anything but it was intimate, as we are best friends. Now that it comes to the right time.

By that means he chose to walk away from his previous relationship. And to be fair, I have held up for a long while before I meet with him again after his break-up. Like a good month long. During that time, we came to a good communication, and understanding, He's one of my best friends. I would hate to lose him to a superficial relationship. And then came the first date, months of temptation were snapped away. That moment that we're both available standing in front of each other. We didn't make it to the dinner, or a date...
We'll take it slow, that is what I told him. But when you try to be in control, the universe tests you. We got into an accident. Pretty fatal, he went into concussion. I still remember how hard it is to not lose my shit on the way to hospital, the fact that he woke up and lost part of his memories. Internal bleeding, brain damage, all the possibilities are running through my head. Is that it? Am I gonna lose my man to an accident just after we have just been together? I prayed to my protector once again. Please allow him to see another light. After all the scans, and monitoring, the doctor allows him to come home. And that was the first day we moved in together. So much for taking it slow....

December

Recovering from a concussion is challenging. Especially, when it happens early on in the relationship. Sometimes I question myself but all relationships require work. And the fact that he's willing to do that with me I'm happy to give it a go. Good communication is the key. As the day goes by, it's Holiday time. Christmas, over the last two years I've been celebrating with the Sanctuary and crews. It only makes sense to celebrate it with them again. As they were in hibernation for so long, it's quite a challenge to pull off a great brunch and dinner. But we did it. Love, sparkling things and bottles of wine. I am exactly where I am supposed to be.

January, 2021

It's a perfect time to reflect back and appreciate the experiences. I'm lucky, if not one of the luckiest people during this crazy time. I lived by the ocean, all those peaceful mornings I woke up to. The gatherings, whilst other places are not allowed to have. Accidents give me lessons that I need to grow. My boyfriend, hmmm and friends who love and hold me through these difficult times. If only I in early 2020 knew where I am now, she won't shed a tear for all those things she thinks she lost. The next thing you know I'm running my own practice, building a new business online, while working on a new relationship. Ain't life a funny thing. I am where I wanted to be.

Once again an old friend of mine reached out to me about her new project... The book. I am no writer, nor have I ever written anything.

But there's no better place to start than here.

Sure, 2020 was my year after all.

Nan Tawunrat Krajaejun

FREYA, 24, DANISH IN INDIA.

A YEAR OF DUALITY.

My light is bright and I serve on this planet as a woman of light and love. I feel this strongly rooted in me, it's a mission I signed up to before coming on this earth. And I will keep remembering myself of this, no matter how many times I can forget. In 2020 I almost forgot my mission. This year has been the most contrast filled year I have experienced. In my earlier life, I haven't experienced many big tragedies nor sorrows. I have always felt invulnerable. But this year I felt heavy darkness for the first time.

I was born in Vietnam and brought up by my Danish mother and her friends in a Christian voluntary organisation and house-sharing community with many children and nationalities. Lots of light! We moved a few times with the organisation; from Vietnam to a year in south Denmark and then a few years in Romania. My mother and I came to Denmark and stayed when I was about six years old; my mother thought it would be good with regular schooling (compared to home-schooling) and a 'normal' lower middle class 'good start' at life. She had been beyond Denmark's borders for the past 20 years, so she often took me out of school for months, so we could go travelling primitively in Asia, most often with the intention of getting involved in voluntary projects. And this traveller, root-less blood is pumping inside of me as well…

So when I finished high-school, I packed my bag and went solo travelling to Nepal and India. AND WEEHEUU! I started my journey and immediately felt the feeling of freedom to be present in the now. To follow the intuition freely and experience flow in a way I have never felt before. To find calmness in not knowing what's next is something I have felt ever since I started my first solo-travels. Countless magical moments, meetings with beautiful souls and encounterings with Spirit have built a massive bonfire in me, which made me believe that I was unshakeable. So much light! At that point, I hadn't encountered darkness yet. 'There is no light without the darkness - one cannot exist without the other'. At this time I didn't realise nor accept this duality and balance.
In the last few years I travelled with a beautiful Argentinian man, living on the road by selling his handmade jewellery. In start January 2020 we went back to India where we met two years before. We went

to Pushkar in Rajasthan for the popular ancient Holi festival at the end of March. Holi is a joyful colourful celebration of spring. Paradoxically in these days of celebrating new life, these were the days where shit hit the fan.

India went in total lockdown from one day to another. Everybody was directed to stay at home, close their businesses and all transportation was shut down across India because of the fear of a total Covid catastrophe in a country where there already was a lack of hospital beds – fortunately, the worst catastrophe scenarios never became a reality. We were directed to stay in lockdown without leaving our guesthouse for an indefinite amount of time. At this time I already had - and continuously have - a strange feeling in my stomach about this whole Covid-situation... I am a system critical rebel by soul who never had much trust in the government, nor the medical and pharma industries. More than the fear of the actual sickness, we all – foreigners as much as the locals – seemed to be more concerned about the possible following consequences…

(Restrictions and rules) the authorities would enforce. We were fortunate to stay in Pushkar, a Hindu city where the locals are very used to foreigners due to the many beautiful temples, the holy lake and the annual Camel Fair. The locals were super helpful despite their fear of the new law enforcements, and we were actually much more concerned about how they would manage this chaotic situation. But it was truly amazing being in such a strongly religious city in the time of crisis - being in a place where their collective belief and prayers are so strongly felt has been such a moving experience. In the beginning, a few times a week, we would run to the roof like everybody else at home and bang pots and pans, yelling full-power "Challo Corona! Challo" which means "Go Corona! Go!". In the evening everybody would light candles on the rooftop, where we would see thousands of lights across the lake and could hear mantras being sung over the speakers. These rituals with intention of healing were super powerful.

We were grateful to have the opportunity to stay at our guesthouse with a family of five, where we were supplied with a kitchen in the garden and they went shopping for us a few times a week. We were approximately 20 people with 16 different nationalities, an amazing mixture of creative beings. We were so grateful to have a beautiful garden, lots of space, big rooftops and an amazing view over the mountains, temples and Pushkar Lake. We called our place "The Golden Cage". Many of us decided to stay to hopefully "ride the wave" for a variety of reasons... Some don't have a regular home to return to. Many didn't have the option to leave; like in my case, the repatriation flights to Denmark were around 2200 euros, so that wasn't an option. Besides, I felt pretty good where I was... Anyhow, we at the guesthouse became super close, referring to each other as family. And I was looking forward to spending my 24th birthday on the 2nd of April together with these colourful close friends.

The 30 of March my friend called me from Denmark, and told me that my best friend, Alfred had intentionally left this life on earth. It is still quite indescribably hard for me – I am still processing this loss of a dear friend. A friend I referred to as my baby brother. This is the first time I've lost a near loved one. I have always had a huge heart for the underdogs, the misunderstood, the rebels. And he was definitely the biggest rebel I knew, a huge inspiration. I remember going to the roof that night on my own and making a little ceremony for him. Burning a candle, singing a few songs, crying, talking to him. I remember ending saying that I forgive him, and that he is free. This loss stayed in my chest as a big stone. Even though I had friends around me, I couldn't seem to allow myself to open up towards these basically new people and deal with all my emotions. I felt very alone. But in some way, I distracted myself from the pain.

At the guesthouse, we were many artists of many kinds; performers, jugglers, musicians, jewellery makers etc. We tried to use time productively, to create and learn throughout these months which seemed like forever. We were doing Spanish lessons, juggling, dancing and Kirtan singing evenings, full moon circles, collective meditations, psychedelic ceremonies, fire spinning performances... We had a fun time and it made us forget that we were in the middle of a so-called "global super-deadly pandemic" which was super surreal. I was improving my poi-skills, my jewellery making skills, painting my first massive wall-painting on our terrace and I was connecting with lots of sweet brothers and sisters. And on a deeper level, I tried not to let my mind and emotions dominate. I tried to push away the negative news media and tried not to fall too deep in my conspiracy rabbit hole, to not let it define my thoughts, emotions and actions in unproductive or self-harming ways. When fear arises from my mind, I need to free myself from my thoughts. I remember myself, that I am not my thoughts and emotions.

In meditation and other spiritual practices, I practice staying in the moment, being in the now. But this year it has been a huge challenge to keep my inner peace.

Sooner or later, we were allowed to roam around town again, but there was still no possibility of leaving the city of Pushkar. We were stuck there in the desert, some days in 45 degrees. Some days felt like we had been there forever and there wouldn't be an end towards all this. Many of us felt like we had been taken away from our freedom and some days the panic and frustration would arise among us. My partner was struggling with the thought of losing his business opportunities, and I felt he didn't have the power to overcome his mind. At some point, I felt a strong calling towards Denmark. I felt like I needed to come home and process the loss of my friend with my closest friends and family, and I felt my mother calling me home. I left India and Pushkar after 5 months and arrived in Denmark in the end of July.

When I arrived back to Denmark, my first mission was to arrange a ceremony for our dear friend although there still were Covid restrictions. It was super healing for our near group of friends, finally being able to gather and to grieve with the loved ones.
Sometimes after a longer amount of time living in foreign countries, the transition was extremely hard for me. My friends and I have a hard time relating to each other because we carry so many other different experiences. And I occasionally feel lonely. In the following months, my relation to my partner started to crumble. We were devastated to be apart from each other and our communication became over emotional and went down a negative spiral. In these months I cried every day, feeling so much anger and frustration, that we didn't know when to see each other again. Suddenly, instead of feeling comfort, I felt scared not knowing what's next. In the end I could not recognise myself in my habit of bad thought-patterns. I needed to refind myself again after this unbearable heaviness I felt and we separated.
The following months went pretty fast. I felt and processed a lot of darkness. I drowned my emotions in alcohol and other substances, which in some way became so destructive, that I paradoxically started to remember my real purpose again. My light mission! In these blurry months, many new angels appeared in my life, showing me back to the paths of light. I've felt a lot of comfort and openness towards me and everything that I contain – not just when I'm shining.

In Denmark there still are a lot of new dictatorial rules and restrictions, which are unjustified and which makes my rebellious blood boil, but I am learning to tame my fire. To use it constructively. There is a movement of people waking up, claiming their rights and freedom. I feel a collective rise of consciousness especially among the younger generations, which gives me hope and again reminds me that I can trust in the way of the universe. I believe and have now felt that true and transformation comes out of destruction of the old. I have understood, but more importantly accepted death and darkness. I have a feeling that these transformative years have just begun, and therefore it seems so important to me, to cultivate and keep my inner peace through rough times. Fix your boat before the storm. For me to radiate my light again and serve my purpose, I need to give myself patience to heal. I am regaining my strength by realising that I can overcome obstacles.

Thank you 2020 for showing me, that I can overcome my mind and emotions by accepting duality, the balance of the universe.

VEDRA, 40 CROATIA.

You can try to lock down the world, but You can never lock down our SPIRITS.

First there was a panic. Basic – Like from what I will live, and what we would eat. After few days it calmed down and I could see clearly. Since at the time when "The Circus" started, I was at my parents place, where we have garden that my grandma use to do, dear, beloved soul.

Well that was it. Like a crazy one, in not more than a week I did everything. From collecting horse manure and preparing the soil, to putting seeds in the ground. It was natural. It was how it was meant to be. Don't think, especially don't over think, just do. Do what your instinct is telling you. After a few weeks when first signs of life started to appear, I knew I'll never be hungry in life. The will, the potential of seeds, water and the warmth of the sun made magic in our garden.

And it was just the beginning. It was March. Time when usually I would return to the seaside and the island I live. But thanks to "The Circus", I stayed with my parents for seven months. The second Renaissance I called it . Sure I could go back. But since they have nice age, since it was whole new situation, I decided to stay and help around. Not for clapping my shoulder, just to be present in the moment, explore, learn, feel. Since I moved out 20 years ago, I didn't spend much time with them. Visiting from time to time, but not like this. If living with other people is challenge, living with my parents was challenge of the challenges.

From laugh to tears, from tears to laugh one million times - It was time where I needed to be there, where I needed to learn how to live with them again. To understand that they don't need me 24/7.

To be able to pack up my van and go off for few days to nature. To recharge so I can come back and be acceptable, for myself and mostly for them. This was the biggest challenge last year gave me.

Though, knowing they won't be around forever, made me more sensitive to the whole situation. Made me realize that we only have what's happening now. And it's up to me/us how we spend it. This was the voice from within, but the real feel was sometimes light years away. The opportunity to grow, to evolve , to love is given to each and every one of us. I'm thankful for last year cos each day we shared lunch together, that we went for walk with mom, that I could give massage to my dad. I'm thankful cos it made me rethink some of my life issues. I'm thankful for the proof that I can grow food. I'm thankful that I could cycle every day next to the river. "The Circus", made misunderstanding between me and one close friend, and we had quarrel. It took me a while to process that, and make connection again, I'm thankful for that. Also I'm thankful when I could finally hit the road, go back to the island, swim at the sea and start to work. Thanks to "The Circus", the season was short. Nevertheless I had nice encounters while giving massages. Unfortunately Ozora fest where I take part in organization didn't happen, and it was strange, after so many years of making festivals, not to be there, surrounded with all those biutiful souls with infinite good energy flow. Thanks to "The Circus", I had even more time for myself. Exploring myself, the island. Hiking in mountains. Making hand craft things. Reading books. Picking herbs and olives. Making jam. Spending time with friends. Looking inside. Who am I in this world? How is affecting me? What I'm expecting from it? What I'm expecting from myself? What should I do to be in peace? Questions arose. Since "The Circus" was omnipresent the smell of panic tried to sneak in from time to time. But, I calmed myself that like everything else, also this will pass. So thanks to last year's changes, now after two month at my parents, I see the difference. When I'm at peace, we all are. When mother is healthy, we all feel it. More understanding, more smiles. For sure there are not so many shiny days, but majority is nice. Father is still building boat. Mother is still knitting. We still share lunch every day, the difference is that now mother is pouring the drinks:) And me, I'm good, I'm very good:) I go to swim, I cycle, make hand crafts. I'm just about to make some major van setup changes. Preparing seeds. In love and just gliding around feeling sky high. Cos I know all is good.

AIMIN, 33 GUATEMALA.

It seemed as if the world had shifted, and I daresay it has.

For my particular story, I will bring you into Guatemala, a land right in the centre of Mesoamerica. The land of many trees and a land of abundant contradictions - amazing landscapes, an awkward political spectrum and a wide variety in cultures.

For me, it began with rumours, not news. And the very first thing I thought about this curious viral outbreak was "scam...something fishy is going on". Though it had started almost 3 months before in China and Europe, the virus reached our continent in March, which is when the quarantine was put in place. I remember it clearly - a weekend full of gigs, one after the other, and very little rest in between. My voice was feeling the strain and I was getting worried I would have to stop singing for some time.

Indeed, I am a singer, a guitarist and a songwriter. I work as a musician in pubs, restaurants, spiritual & healing ceremonies, yoga classes, weddings, festivals, and whatever provides me with income and varying degrees of fun and stimulation. Two not so different lands provide me with the most work – Antigua, amidst a valley nestled between three imposing volcanoes – and Lake Atitlán, a lake protected by a fantastical mountain range and another three imposing volcanoes. What are the odds?

So the famous weekend where the world changed arrived. Several gigs were crammed into the weekend, and I was once again travelling to and fro between Antigua and Atitlán. The income obtained then seemed to warn me of an impending doom in which I would need some savings to make it through - obviously enough, that's what happened. I mean, it's not as if I had no clue that quarantine was going to happen. It was a subject of talk and discussion - when was the country going to close? How much more time did we have to prepare? But sometimes, we don't want to believe in these things, simply because we don't want it to happen or maybe because we are on a winning streak. And I could swear I was on one.

Half the people were already using a mask to cover their nose and mouth, but I still couldn't see myself doing such a thing. I finally returned home to Antigua and rested. After hearing of Antigua's first case, it was obvious now that businesses would shut down and the country would soon be under quarantine and curfew. And so it was - reality had changed completely from one day to the next. Some people were afraid, most were paranoid, and a few were taking it as a long awaited pause to the rat race. I was one of those relieved world citizens, feeling a sudden drop in activity and a rising peace in the air. This had never happened before and I had hoped for such a thing. Maybe there was hope for humanity, after all.

I will not lie and say I didn't get the paranoid vibe for a day or two, but it was only because I suddenly felt the flu coming, and I foolishly told my house mates how I felt. Of course, everyone got paranoid and basically ordered me to go get a test, which was impossible since hospitals were only receiving people who were really sick. So, we all relaxed and tried to carry out a sense of normality and routine in order to keep each other positive and active.

Every day of the three weeks I spent in our secluded mountain paradise was magical, and I constantly felt amazed at the relief I felt all around. The birds sang clearer, the air blew more pure, and the collective mind was quieter. A sense of adventure lay in my heart and I knew things would soon change radically. The great mystery was "how?"

I then received a strong message to join my parents for at least a couple weeks of quarantine and I followed the hunch. My stay ended up stretching to a month and it ended up being a necessary thing - our eyes finally met in peace and acceptance, and our relationship started to change, to heal. I finally understood how the family can be a team and also a refuge when we need it. I had been absent from these sweet family dynamics for too long.

Throughout my stay, I was talking to a lovely friend I had met only two months before. She lives in a special town in mystical Lake Atitlán called Santiago, which I had once dreamt of living at. Through daily chats and messages, our connection grew and the distance slowly become an obstacle for the desire and love we felt for one another. I was now practically inhabiting three different homes - the one I had rented for 3 years, my parents' home, and the one that was calling me in from the mystical Lake Atitlán.

After the wholesome visit I paid my parents, I returned to my own place for my last few weeks of solitude. Saying goodbye to my housemates wasn't as hard as I expected. It's as if life knew the magic and joy that awaited me so it just nudged me on towards my next destination.

I still had to wait a couple of weeks before I could finally dive into the main adventure. I returned to my parents' home for one last transition, and it wasn't easy to take the leap out. I was still hesitant and unclear. But I was falling in love...

After a bit of drama and tension within, I took the golden opportunity that the Universe had prepared for me. Ellie would be waiting for me in her magical adobe in the middle of the Atitlán country, and I would come to her, choosing to follow my heart and that hunch I had felt before.

I arrived with no work, a tiny bit of money, and a heart full of hope. I was jumping into an adventure with a woman I had known for very little, in the most weird of times, and to the most magical of lands. Furthermore, Santiago Atitlán's Covid situation was very interesting and strict – they closed off the entrance into town and no one could come inside or leave. I was really lucky to have been (boy)friend to a woman who worked in public health – boxes of medicines were needed every 3 months or so, and the date I managed to get inside, I was part of the transport that brought the medicine!

The feeling of living an adventure was always present and the restrictions of quarantine and forced refuge further deepened the sensation. Those four hours I travelled were possibly the most magical I ever experienced on the road. A growing tension formed inside of me, wondering if I would even be allowed to come inside the protected perimeter. I had no way of knowing either if I would get along well with Ellie or not. The most potent of ingredients came together - uncertainty, love, passion, isolation, fear, and adventure. And the rain! The heavy amount of rain always present, accompanying the views and cleaning the unease away.

I arrived after dusk, and the rain continued. Ellie received me with tenderness, love and the most delicious dinner ever. In the days after, things ran smoothly and I easily found a home with her. Our love grew and it became clear that the two of us were meant to go through these times together. I started doing all the things that I had wanted to but hadn't gotten myself to do - working with the earth, planting, preparing probiotic healthy food, and really tuning into my body. I healed my wounded hand, I understood how to manage my crippling back pains, and I found a couple of keys that began teaching me how to successfully navigate the musical world. All this while opening my heart like never before and navigating a beautiful relationship that was slowly taking flight.

I really feel that I was initiated into a greater version of myself. Things weren't always smooth or easy and they were never superficial - the experiences that happened went deep into my body, my heart and my spirit. Once again, nature healed and guided me home. The rawness of the primal and magical energy in the lake served as a playground for my Awakened Spirit – I started manifesting my true self and the conditions to thrive in.

I found out that our personal lives are not separate from our professional lives - they are both different sides of life - and that the way to have balance is to understand that by heading towards harmony in our personal space we will head towards harmony in our professional spaces. I definitely had to think outside the box and deeply feel what was going on inside. It was a lot of inner work, but I had the aid of what I call "ally substances", and I managed to mix fun, inner work, psychedelia, heart openings, focus, inspiration and productivity. Even an aspect of my life and an attribute I had shunned for 7 years came back with full force - teaching.

If you are inspired constantly, are connecting deeply to your skills and are aligning to your mission, chances are you'll teach, share and tell of what you have learnt throughout life. In my case, music has been the one constant and the greatest vehicle for healing, growing and maturing. The turn for teaching my lovely luggage of musical knowledge and intuition certainly came. Clarity returned. Joy entered my heart and found a steady and reliable home. I fiercely and lovingly believe that music, artistic expression and transparency/vulnerability are powerful tools for transformation.

I knew that before, but I didn't have the confidence to walk through life with that clarity as my compass. Now I do! Now I am deeply connected to my music, to divinity, my ancestors, to the earth and to the family I created with my partner, her dog, my dog and our cat. 2020 was a blessing and 2021 is yet another even grander blessing. I don't have any more doubts, I still have many ideas, and I am constantly grateful and inspired. The songs that I've channelled through the lockdown are making their way into an album filled with "messenger songs". Life is good...challenging...but so, so good.

Take the lesson that life, God(ess) and the Universe present to you...and be sure that you will revolutionise it all.

RUSTY, 50, USA CITIZEN IN CHINA.

CHINA AND QUARENTINE.

I write to you about my experience of being locked up through quarantine. This story really is that I somehow didn't experience this crazy thing that has been happening all around the world for the past year. Living in Shanghai China, we had a time which was around three weeks of actual quarantine and then three months of fear induced SELF-quarantine. My girlfriend didn't leave her apartment for 6 weeks. Her grandparents for three months. When China's government talks and commands the people listen and more.

During the actual quarantine in March last 2020, I was in a crazy situation where I had this city of 35 MILLION people to myself. I visioned that it was a movie about apocalypse and everyone was gone except me. I rode my bike backwards down the highways, I went through all the tunnels that are off limit to bicycles. I just simply rode my bike....All day, all night. There wasn't any one around! Not even police, No taxis, No people. Nothing was open! I loved it. I lived in a big four bedroom apartment that is usually filled with vibrant young expats from all around the world and no one was around. I loved it! Netflix and peace and quiet.

China rebounded quite fast because they quickly closed all borders. With over a billion people, they really don't need outside help financially. This BOOMING economy just flows, spends and shops. They have online sites that make more money than Amazon and eBay COMBINED in one year, they make more money in ONE DAY! Look it up...Alibaba or Toabao!

I must talk about BLAME and usually when I point my finger there is a saying that: "what ONE finger points at...THAT...THREE fingers point back at me". I am a blamer, and always wanted to know why and who is responsible. In USA now there is crazy Asian violence and brutality towards some people that look Asian and haven't even left USA....born and raised. (I am one of those people born in Vietnam and half asian, so i find this crazy… but hey, Americans are filled with guns fear and violence)

Stop blaming! Stop wondering who started and know we are a collective, we are one unit of humans that live on Mother Earth and she will do as she pleases. Viruses have been around LONGER than humans. Viruses will continue to be the cleaning house of the human species. Weaker gets lost and stronger survive! Where did it start.........EARTH!

I'm really sorry for the rest of the world where people are having no money, lost jobs, depression, fear, death and what not...STILL these restrictions that leave you ANGRY. I don't blame you! But I can't write about any of that because I hit the jackpot for being in the right place at the right time. China has absolutely been such a great experience to live here through this pandemic. I got jobs right away with personals since I am a yoga teacher and breathwork trainer and facilitator. My workshops were filled to capacity by June 2020. Studios open by July and Teacher trainings started my August.
Blessed!
Life takes us up and down and you can never know your future. We just have to be present and receptive to what is given every moment. Grateful for our lives and health.
I actually don't know ANYONE here in China that has gotten Covid! Not one family member in three families in USA have gotten Covid! I know a few from Europe that have had extreme stress and weak immune systems and they got it but lived. Covid, the 2020 and so on game changer in our human history. Clears the weak and make more room for the fit! So, please, use this time to deep breath, do yoga, workout and be kind to yourself. You will live longer and feel more positive. Love your life... I love mine EVERY SECOND and you can also!

Much love Rusty

BEN, 37 LEEDS UK.

It's interesting timing that I'm writing this now, opposed to a couple of weeks ago... You see, lockdown for me has been such a Beautiful Struggle...

Just 2 weeks prior to this I had zero food in my cupboards other than rice and some black pepper n seasoning. Yet in this moment, as my stomach screamed in hunger, my gratitude went towards not having to experience this each n every day…

How in '21 can poverty be such a prominent regularity of a common position for people of these shores to be in? And, then, there lies part of the problem – why is it a shock when it now happens and affects those of us in the UK? When this has affected two-thirds of the World for decades upon decades each and every day... No families or no person with the resources this Planet produces should have to suffer and be starved of basic essentials based on their financial credentials – to me that's criminal! We as human beings should be given the decency to live and not be forced to forage for survival.

It really is vital to think that people with families to feed have to struggle like this constantly. It's so harrowing - no one should have to suffer the pain of hunger, but even more so, it shouldn't be as widespread accepted or rather overlooked as it is.

The irony here though is what has fuelled my entire mindset throughout the last year, has been the hunger to level up, transform and see this as an opportunity to reset with the Planet, rather than see it as pause.

I remember the last weekend before the initial lockdown came into effect. I was DJin in Manchester and it was an amazing atmosphere, a real special energy and a night to savour under any average circumstances, but even more so due to its significance pre-empting what followed - which is a complete collapse of my revenue income stream, alongside my dream career and vocation being withdrawn literally overnight.

A lot of doubt and worry arose – how was I gonna be able to support myself or pay my rent...

These were further compounded by watching a brilliant tv show from the last decade called Utopia, which had so many parallels to this pandemic it made me really allow helplessness to set in; which then led to some grave-ly dark thoughts, that I had only a year ago, celebrated getting over by speaking about my experience - of reaching and climbing out from rock bottom during my set of my first ever Stand Up Comedy World Tour in '19.

For me to return to these thoughts felt like the rug of my grounded World had been pulled from underneath me.

Fortunately though my inner resolve quickly, after an intense 18 hours, pulled through and built an impenetrable base from within which has proved to be my permanent building block to grow from. You see, in those 18 hours, I endured a grief that had to be felt and experienced so it could dissolve rather than suppress – and that was the best course of action, as that eradicated any fraction of doubt of what it is I'm truly about...it wasn't fear, it was Faith! Understanding our UnIverse is, has n always will be my Best Mate!

So even though this fate wasn't the one I chose, it allowed me to keep on my toes... It showed a mirror to my insecurities... allowed me to acknowledge my priorities... and paved the way for fresh opportunities... although I'm not gonna lie - chocolate mushrooms really also helped along this trip – hahahaha!

A true release along with a set intention and this matched with my Faith, now led me to be at One with Divine Creation!

My salvation came in my Creative outlet...

Meaning more than simply my vocation, this was me able to connect with people far n wide. First by doing a quiz, I then went on and launched an Instagram Chat Show called 'Loose Lips'! It gave me a purpose but also set me a chance to uplift the Spirits of both guest and viewer. It kept me ready and taught me new skills such as editing (which sucks by the way - haha) plus the overall body of work is timeless and the content from the chats is priceless!

Then lockdown lifted and I managed to fit in a night out for my Birthday! Remember them rare things, a night out…

Me n a mate also set ourselves the task to write a short film comedy script and film it, which we did. I began a radio show n things were looking up, until the shitty wank tiers fucked the hospitality industry even further, as according to these melts in gov 10.00pm curfews and booze with food is somehow a cure battling the virus.

Then another lockdown came after this! Sheer tier'ranny followed by tiers that was code for yet another lockdown, as Chrimbo came n went, n plus my beloved Arsenal had been shite after winning the FA Cup - n everything just felt like meh... as yet another lockdown came to greet in the New Year.

We were glad to see the end of 2020 which could do one, as we are so done, but then it wasn't exactly the start we wanted for '21... and this third lockdown felt like groundhog day - and this one felt like groundhog day; and this one felt like groundhog day; and this one felt like groundhog day!

And then just as no end was in sight, I leant on my Faith – "this ain't to last" – I told myself "this ain't to last" – "this ain't to last" - "this ain't to last" and like George Harrison my favourite Beatle once said "all things must pass"!

I can feel the shift in energy to our New Age!

I felt that I was able to focus on my creative pursuits further, as I sorted my tunes out and added to my sick collection so my DJ sets are gonna be even more special occasions. I finished my first draft of my second Stand Up Special! I feel ahead in my planning, and all of this, while recently reaching the stage of having no food in for a week, compiled by the realisation of having no gigs or getting to do what I love for an entire year – to say how I started lockdown to now be in this position of appreciation and gratitude, matched with patience and reverence for what this next chapter and stage has in store, is really what my hunger fuelled! I'm overjoyed and bursting with excitement to showcase what I've been developing – it's gonna blow people away and Spark the Soul of Our Generation!

Truth is though, I wouldn't wish this time to happen again or for anyone and it makes me think of all those who've not had their creativity to fall back on... or those who've lost loved ones or had significant days taken from them! And this whole experience has allowed me to broaden my perspective – this ain't forever – however, my optimistic Energy, Spirit and Power is and my role is to uplift those who don't have that strength, too boost them to find it within themselves - and this is what my creations during this time have been fuelled by.

I feel more community is on the horizon alongside our freedom. Seeing and joining the Black Lives Matter protests in the last 2020 summer showed a collective unity! The needle on the record of Life has moved to a deeper groove and it's about flowing with this rhythm breeding daily Harmony. As the music is in everyday Life encounters, and we surely must be tuned in to the beat of peace after this by being more thoughtful and considerate n I, for one, am up for it.

Our experiences over the last 12 months are as personal as they are commonplace, and, when it all picks back up - I do feel capitalism will wane for compassion below the surface.

So yeah, that's me - Ben Brown aka Ben Randm, who's lived a lockdown with my ace cat Princess Sheila Rascal offering you a brief glimpse into our sanctuary amongst the lunacy.

It's been nowhere near as brutal as it has been for others, but it very well could have been... but I didn't let it get to me how it set out initially... n I'm Forever Proud of who I've grown into during this cocoon in human history…

Now it's my time to fly and my wings are gonna have an immeasurable, impactful, important and immaculately immense impression on our Planet, in our Worlds across the Globe and beyond our UnIverse. As a Beacon of Light to Guide us through from the storm to calmer shores away from this Beautiful Struggle...

Peace & Light #benrandm

RUBA, 37, PALESTINE/SAUDI IN MONT-REAL.

Since I agreed to write this chapter, I have been living with an enormous sense of anger and fury, the likes of which, I've never felt before.

Truth is, this experience has been one of the hardest things I've ever had to do. I started and re-started writing the chapter four times. Nothing of what I wrote felt right. The whole process was heavy, and all the words sounded very artificial, as if I'm telling a story that is not mine. And then it hit me, I am telling a story that is not mine, for I am no longer the same person.

The person I once was, had died. That part of me doesn't exist any-more, except in memory and in fear. I realised the anger, the fury and my inability to write come from the same place - mourning. I never mourned the loss of my old self. A person lived an entire life, and I just wanted to zoom through to the next chapter as if that life didn't matter. As if all that passed was a burden and I was all but ready to sweep it under the proverbial rug and forget all about 'Her'.

If I have learned anything this past year, it's how chaotic life can get. I lost five family members in the span of five months. I couldn't see or say goodbye to any of them before they died. I lost friends as I became 'too weird' in quarantine.

I navigated an ending marriage, while being locked in the same space with the man. And for the very first time in four years, I actually spent time with my son. I got to see the world through the eyes of a of a kid living with Sensory Processing Disorder (SPD). A life where everything is messy, everyone is loud, and nothing makes any sense.

Trying to write about a messy life in a 'pretty and presentable' way is wasted effort. So, I decided to write my past self a eulogy, to commemorate the moment my old life ended, to honor my pain and to validate the experiences I lived this past year, in lockdown.

Ruba Al Ghoul (May 22nd 1984-February 27th, 2021)

Montreal, Canada

"This is who I am". ~ Oprah Winfrey

Where do I start describing the life of Ruba Al Ghoul, who passed away peacefully on Feb. 27th, 2021, at the age of 37, at home in Montreal, after a lifelong battle with self-doubt, clinical depression, systematic social (Arabic), religious (Muslim) and familial pressures and abuse.

And how do I celebrate a whole life in a few brief words that is more appropriately told in a book or a screenplay? The answer is simple - as I always wanted it told.

I, Ruba- a.k.a. mother, lightworker, Prism and Divine being, passed only hours after having a conversation with Death during the full moon breathwork session I participated in, earlier that day.

I was very busy during the last decade: I got married; got pregnant; lost the pregnancy after three months; got pregnant again; lost the second pregnancy at four months; my marriage started collapsing; got pregnant again; was put on bed rest for eight month; took over 500 hormone injections to keep the pregnancy, before finally giving birth to a son in 2016.

In March of 2020, my life hit a new low after I lost my job and was forced to become fully dependent on a husband, who by now, felt like a total stranger, and social security, for the first time in decades.

I spent the last year searching for self and soul. Three days after being let go from work, I went on a journey of a lifetime to Peru, and found God inside the Plant Medicine Ayahuasca, at the foot of Mount Ollantaytambo in Cusco Peru.

I also cured my clinical depression and severe anxiety disorder, when I sat down, for the first time with myself, and took a deep breath in. I found the power of breathwork and my life changed from that point on.

There, I discovered how resilient and capable I was, after becoming severely ill due to accidental poisoning. I was hospitalised for days, all by myself, a stranger in a strange land. Yet, I had no doubt that somehow, everything would turn out alright - and it did.

After returning home, I began the hardest chapter of my life. I went on to learn the magic of Dynamic breathwork at the hands of a gift-ed Healer. She took me on a journey of generational wound healing, spirit mending and mind bending beyond anything I could have imagined.

I learned all about ascension and shadow work. I went through the most healing journey into my soul. I became an expert on the Pain body and moving trauma out with toning.

In the months that followed, I dove deep into my wounded child with the help of another magnificent woman, who taught me how to forgive and love all the parts of myself, even when I really didn't want to.

When the rest of the world was panicking, I was learning how to find my inner peace. Every time I felt lost, scared or just about ready to quit, I picked up my camera, or a book, or a paint brush. I replaced trauma with knowledge and envy with inspiration. I discovered how great a mother I am and stepped so much outside of my anxiety and started sharing my life with my child and the world.

My death made way for someone brand new, someone who is actively choosing not to be attached to any outcome, who doesn't project, someone living deliberately and with purpose.

It taught me that we all die many times in a lifetime, and this process is endlessly fascinating and achingly beautiful. I learned to forgive quickly and be kind, to others and to self. I learned how to cultivate gratitude; believe in magic; be of service and generous; do whatever it takes to stay out of the mind; and most importantly, I learned to let go, relax, and to have fun.

ANDREA & JOHN, RETIRED UK CITIZENS IN TURKEY.

I cannot believe a year has gone by and the pandemic is still around.

I first heard about the Corona virus in China in January 2020 – I watched the news reports, showing people infected with the virus, taken from their homes and away from their loved ones. I never dreamt anything like that could happen in our part of the world. My home is in Dalyan in Turkey...

In February I had to go to England to visit my mum. Whilst there, I heard that Covid 19 had arrived in the UK, entering the country by people returning from holiday at a Swiss ski resort. More news circulated that worried me and my husband, concerned that they might stop our return flights to Turkey. Lucky for us we got back! Big relief as we feel safer in Turkey than in the UK.

We had moved there a few years back after retiring from working hard our whole adult life... We both noticed a gradual change in quality of life in the UK, mostly since the financial crisis in 2006... People seemed to be more and more money driven. This made us re-evaluate things and take the risk to sell up and move.

We had visited Dalyan for many years previous... and we loved it!

It is a small village by the sea, with hot sunshine most of the year round, good food and beautiful, kind people. The pace of life is much slower, we have no use for a car and it felt like being back in the 70s. We are in heaven.

Here, we are so isolated from big city life - we never imagined the virus from china reaching us here, not in this small paradise, but it did.

March 8th came - That was my husband, John's birthday, which we celebrated with about 50 friends at one of our favourite restaurants, Nazos. All was normal and a good time was had by all. But by the following week, we heard of increasing corona virus cases in Turkey. Along came our first lockdown - not allowed out at weekends and over 65s were completely housebound. As I am under 65, I was allowed out to shop or exercise. So I had to do all the shopping. I used my bike to get around, and wore a face mask and gloves. My glasses would steam up and the shopping was heavy, but I managed. We also washed all items that we brought into the house. Even though cases in Turkey were low, under twenty per week - all precautions had to be observed and tourists were not allowed into the country.
John was secretly loving his retired lockdown status I think... He loved his own company and feels it even benefited him physically - to

have all that rest after a very demanding work life all those years in the UK. He seemed more at peace, allowing him to just do nothing and be still, with our 3 cats Fluff, Luki, and Kuki for all those weeks, he literally went nowhere!

With very low numbers in our area, by June /July, over 65s were allowed out, but had to be back home by 8pm. Tourists were allowed back with no restrictions – they did not obey any rules, such as the wearing of masks etc, which caused friction between them and the locals. Therefore we kept to bars and restaurants only used by locals and did not go near tourist areas.

So for peak of summer we were able to carry on with boat trips, going to the beach and lazy days by our pool. Not bad at all.

Back in England, my siblings were concerned for our mum. She was being shielded and was not having any visitors apart from food drops and my daughter going to sit with her in the garden. Worried and unable to help from so far away, I carried on with our usual daily chats on the phone, sometimes more than once a day, to try and keep mum in a good state of mind. She did not really understand what was going on and thought we used it as an excuse not to visit. It was so hard for the older generation to get their heads around it all.

Even for myself, it was so surreal. If you told me years ago that this could happen, I would not believe it.

Then news came one morning late in July that mum had had a stroke and ended up in hospital, added to which, she was only allowed one visitor, my sister Dianne. I wanted to go, but was told they would not let me see her, so there was no point even trying. Plus we were nervous to fly, hearing so much on the news of spreading cases.
Dianne was visiting her every day in hospital, and nothing else could be done at this stage. Due to the rules concerning her isolation from us, it was difficult to understand the severity of her condition, and we all just assumed that she would at least get well enough to leave hospital and return to her home in Balderton, near Newark.

September came and I had a visit from my daughter, Lisa, which was so nice. I had a small birthday party at a local restaurant.
In Dalyan we are surrounded by so much nature, mountains, lakes and beaches... so it was easy to forget what was going on in the world, as we enjoyed the hot sunshine.

Then, I got the call I never wanted, saying "come back asap, if you want to see mum" - she didn't have much time left and had stopped eating. So I immediately booked a flight for the next day.

The hospital had moved mum into a nursing home without the family's consent. We were distraught but again had to make peace with the rules as no amount of stress could have changed anything. Then, due

to corona virus, they had put her in quarantine for 2 weeks. 10 days into the quarantine was when we got this dreaded call. And even then, she was only allowed one visitor at a time and max two people in any one day. On the day I was flying to the UK my brother Tony, and sister Dianne were allowed to see her for the first time since she'd left the hospital. Dianne got them to allow a third person for my visit, but they changed their minds and we had to insist they let me in to see her. Thank god they did, as I was then able to spend time with her on my own, whilst Dianne had no choice but to wait in the car, not allowed inside due to the care home's restrictions.
I was shocked when I walked into the room and saw how poorly she had become, only a skeleton of her old self. It took me a while to come to terms with what was happening and after a good cry, I spoke to her - held her hand and stroked her hair. I told her how beautiful she was and how nice her hair felt. I soothed her and said it's me Mum, Andrea. I've come home. I noticed her look at me and squint a little trying to focus on me and it felt like she knew I was there and acknowledged my presence. She was glad to see me, although she could not communicate. I kissed her and told her to relax - all was well and how we all love her. I told her, her granddaughter was coming on the following day to see her and that Dianne was outside. To comfort her I told her not to worry and relax - all her family loved her and that my Dad was looking down on us all. I said prayers with her and spoke about her Mum, my Babcia and her family. So much

time passed I did not want to leave her, but eventually had to and promised that I would be back. I asked to speak to the nurse and asked how close Mum was to the end and she said that it wasn't easy to say, but they would know from experience to give us plenty of warning for the family to be there when the time came. Unfortunately they did not which made me angry, but maybe Mum realised she had already said her goodbyes to her three children and could be at peace.

Mum passed away that night. But, because of their rules, my sister had not been allowed to see her mum for two days. I saw her just the once on her last day – our brother, Anthony also the day before. Stupid rules! I will never forgive them. My daughter, Lisa was going to visit that Sunday but unfortunately it was too late.

The funeral was sad of course but quite joyful, as even with the Covid rules we finally managed to get quite a few of her friends and family together... although it was strange to be wearing masks and standing the required distance apart.

In many ways I feel she left at the right moment; it was on a special day in the Jewish calendar - although we are not Jewish but catholic; we found out that it was a special day to pass over.

And now she is back with my Dad who had left her a long time before... she had missed him so much. Her last years had been difficult and I'm happy she's now at rest.

As soon as we could my husband and I returned to Turkey, because again there was talk of stopping flights. We had two flights cancelled before managing to get one from Birmingham. The airport was spooky, almost empty with hardly any travellers in sight.
Back home we could relax... with plenty of time to grieve, and as they say, "Life goes on". And now I want to make the most of every moment. I miss my mum and dad every day, but now they live on through me and I choose to enjoy this precious life!!

YVETTE, 41 MELBOURNE.

It was February 2020, Melbourne where I met Camilo, an extremely handsome, intelligent and emotionally sound Colombian, who was amazing at salsa. I had never had much luck with men in my 40 years of life, but it was the moment I'd finally found my match. We were at the St Kilda festival and unbeknown to us it was the last large gathering we would attend in almost a year. The connection was undeniable and we soon realised how much we had in common, our political views were similar and we just wanted to live and contribute to a more equitable world. I didn't know it then but having this man by my side was going to be the lifeline I needed to get me through one of the most difficult times in my life.

In March 2020, I had planned to go to Bali and meet my younger sister Nicole who was holidaying in Thailand. I was hearing about COVID-19 but at that stage I didn't consider it a threat, it just seemed so abstract! I guess I was in denial, I thought "they will contain it" and "it won't happen to us". However, I started receiving personal reports from friends in Italy and France, they sent videos of army tanks patrolling the streets and that's when it started to sink in just how serious this was.

We had a family group chat on Whatsapp with my Mum, brother and two sisters. There was talk of how the virus is a tool used to collapse the economy a term coined "Plandemic". With reference to Donald Trump's tweet on 10 March 2020, "So last year 37,000 Americans died from the common Flu... Nothing is shut down; life and the economy go on". Also, how pensioners are mostly affected so according to my brother, "I don't think it's going to be the worst thing in the world if a bunch of old people die and taxes go down". It was becoming apparent that my views were in stark contrast to those of my family, which saddened me deeply. However, at this stage we were all managing to be respectful towards each other.

The Australian government announced a travel ban and the trip to Bali was cancelled. Deep down I was quietly pleased about it because I was in the midst of falling deeply in love and the thought of leaving Camilo behind was unbearable. I started tuning into the news and I felt anxiety creep in. I wanted to know more about the virus but, no matter how many articles I read, it didn't bring any of the clarity I was seeking it only induced more fear.

I started to change my behaviour before lockdown was announced opting to ride my bike to university instead of using public transport. I arranged for most of my food to be delivered. I avoided supermarkets until it was absolutely necessary and, when I did stock up before lock-down, the sight of empty shelves moved me to tears. I started to feel like the world, as I knew it, was ending. I had been trying to stay positive and avoid the reality of it all but, to tell you the truth, I was beyond scared. Now with lock-down an uncomfortable and unfamiliar feeling washed over me as I realised I have no control over what the future holds. No more making plans, booking holidays, going to restaurants or festivals - all of the things I once took for granted just wasn't possible anymore.

The initial panic dissipated quickly as I adjusted to life in isolation which, to my surprise I actually enjoyed. My studies moved online and I enjoyed my daily walks in the park. I also took some distance from the family chat as I realised I needed to focus on the things I could control. I became increasingly aware of my vibration while going down the rabbit hole of conspiracy theories, COVID-19 facts, rising fatalities and news reports from around the world. I had to make a conscious choice to break free from a fear based mindset as I was aware of how it was bringing me down energetically. So, instead of tuning into the news or some information my family had sent in the chat, I found things to be grateful for like being healthy, appreciating sunshine and nature on my walks.

I was fortunate enough to live in a beautiful apartment without housemates who could potentially affect my mental and physical well-being. With domestic violence and suicides on the rise I couldn't deny how lucky I was to have my own space. All the worst possible scenarios I had been playing out in my head, thank-fully didn't eventuate – like catching this disease and dying and running out of food supplies. As much as this pandemic was a worldwide disaster, I felt a little guilty taking pleasure in the pause, as it paved the way for Camilo and I to spend quality time together – connecting without distractions, in some strange way it was a blessing for us.

However there were challenging times - I missed the social interaction at university and the family chat was becoming increasingly negative and low vibration. Until one day the resurgence of the Black Lives Matter movement following George Floyds death sparked a confrontation. My mother mentioned that the movie "Gone with the wind" had been removed from HBO, which caused a lot of anger amongst some family members. It is an American movie produced in the 1930's during the segregation period of whites and people of colour in the South of the United States.

I asked a question merely to start a conversation regarding the racist stereotypes and themes in the movie only to be met with an aggressive voice message from my brother "If you stand for this you're a piece of shit mate..... Who the fuck are you cunt? You need to pull your head in!" The point I was trying to make had been totally misinterpreted, it was as if I was speaking another language, I felt completely misunderstood. However, I felt there was no point in continuing the conversation and I left the group. I believe that racial disparity is an important topic to talk about and it's something that has always been close to my heart. Also now with my partner being Colombian and having African heritage it's further opened my eyes to the historical oppression and current systemic racism that is still very much alive today.

The next day my sister Mary, posted a facebook clip claiming that racism doesn't exist and I commented - only to be publicly bullied by my brother and others. There was so much anger and hate towards anyone who believed racism did exist. I came to realise that, instead of this being an issue regarding humanity, it had quickly turned political. I was never interested in US politics, however it is something Camilo is extremely passionate about, so I learnt a lot about the various parties and the characteristics of the extreme Right and Left which I now know is valuable knowledge to have if you want to make some impact in the world.

Over the months as mask wearing became mandated and curfews were introduced the pressure of the situation started mounting. I understand that it was a difficult time but what was happening within the family was only making a hard situation worse. At around the 6 month mark of lock-down things seemed hopeless and I hit a really low point. I started to see a psychologist who started to help me understand my childhood traumas and learn the lessons from them, so as not to repeat them. Camilo was also a huge support for me he was always there listening, trying to understand and offer guidance. When I met him I had a wall up so high that it was hard for people to get to know the real me. In between the first and second lockdown we moved in together, which increased the trust between us. I slowly began to soften and feel safe around him. We decided to start trying for a baby but I was struggling with my physical health and I believe the stress played a big part.

I think the turning point for me was when I had my first ever panic attack - I was trying to get my Mum to talk to me, but I was shut out. Then I realised that I just have to let this family stuff go. I was too caught up in trying to prove myself and get them to understand me, but it was just further damaging relationships and causing me to turn into this crazy person. My family was acting more like a biker gang, where you have to be loyal even if someone in the pack does something that isn't morally right. A functional family embraces each other's individuality, but it was clear that the only way I was going to receive love and acceptance from my family was to conform to their values and beliefs. Therefore, I had no choice, if I wanted to be authentic to myself and speak about the issues that are on my heart, I had to spend time with the people who want to have those conversations with me.

This pandemic created the conditions for massive controversy, arguments, fear, pain and struggle. However, as there is light in any dark situation, it also created the conditions for transcendence and awakening. Thanks to the pause of lockdown I was able to tune into my own unique guidance system, and navigate through the shadows of my past. I finally found my voice and the courage to express myself and, although it came with consequences, it helped me realise who I am - what is important, what I stand for and what I need to let go of. I'm still here, I'm not broken and I couldn't be happier.

Meanwhile Camilo and I are having fun dancing and still trying to make a baby! This whole situation tested us and only solidified our commitment and love for each other. The pandemic taught us courage, resilience and adaptability. Without COVID-19 it may have taken years to know what we now know about each other and it definitely made us stronger. No matter how terrible any situation is, if you look hard enough there is always a silver lining. As Freud once said, "One day in retrospect, the years of struggle will strike you as the most beautiful."

FIONA, 55 SOUTH AFRICA.

Lockdown

Down at the tip of Africa

Africa the forgotten

Forget the "people" is the policy of the ANC

cANCer government - self-serving, self-funding, selfish

Fishing for finance in every corner possible

Possibilities for people - NO - We offer 15 pound, sterling to those unemployed

A Ploy to steal more - take more - fill greedy pockets

Pick pocketing rife - how do I feed myself, my family, my children

Children without food, education, resources, roofs

A roof over my head she cries, evicted at 72, on the street with her cat

"Catch my dog if he runs away" says the Madam to the dog-walker

Walking dogs was my life, and now I have no job - I hang myself from the tree outside the church

Church soup kitchens feeding the homeless - gathering daily

"Please sir, can I have some more"?

More fear, fear, fear… and now tears, tears, tears
Tears for those I saw or spoke to just days or hours ago
Ago! Ago and boom, they gone
How did that happen I gasp?
Gasping for air, I can't breathe says the American Black Lives Matter
Matter of fact - just another day in Africa - black, white, grey - what is colour anyway
Anyway - we listen to Cyril - Cyril is our Man, but actually just a puppet
Puppets dance to the song of corruption
"Jerusalema" our new song of hope
Hope for a cure, Hope for something new
New dawns and new days
A Daze of dissociation as each flows past a year
A year to be... to A and now Zee
See, I can breathe now... I can soften into a new way
Way beyond my dreams or nightmares
Night and day flow into and out to
Today I sing into my exhale
Exhale and inhale, and yes I'm alive
Lives matter as I walk the path to offer food
Food of nourishment and food of wisdom

Food of forgiveness

Forgive ... it's time we say as we see

Sea embrace me, cleanse me, show me

It's not all about me... and now I see

See and seek and bypass this sickness

Nest me in your heart

Hear me in your pulse

Pulse on, pulse on, pulse on

OZGITA, 43 TURKEY.

Who could possibly ever think this would happen? I wouldn't! The film scenarios did get real... so many stories along the way. It is going to be one year now almost...

Just before the quarantine started, I went to Izmir where my mom lives on the Aegen coast of Turkey. I went for another reason and I had to stay there. Turkey and specially Izmir, is a country with the Mediterrean mentality and so it was much easier where we were. Some days I questioned if the the virüs was real, because outside people weren't paying attention at all. It was almost like before except for the weekends, and my mom was totally relaxed. Wearing masks even lasted a month :) and it was March , beginning of the spring time - the smell of the orange blossoms were blowing my mind - the dancing perfumes of all the flowers in the air…

And at the same time, so many people were dying and so much fear on earth. People were desperate - a tiny virüs which cannot be seen with bare eyes - a threat to every single person on the planet without separating language, race, colour, nationality, rich, poor is the most democratic attitude I've ever seen. I did also go through it and what I exprienced was the most amazing thing. During the 2 weeks time of the illness, whenever I got really sad and hopeless my fever was rising. And whenever I pulled myself up, did my breathwork and meditation I was getting better. Breathwork did lower my fever every time I did it...

But my story is a love story as they are always more close to me than the reality - this one is a sad one. Because we are separated after all this period. Who knows if Corona plays a role in this. Maybe helped us in a way to set our lives how we really wanted them to be. So many awakening moments for the ones who stayed alive. It was the strangest time for partners. Some got really more intimate and some had enough and separated.

So I was understanding in what kind of psychology and mindset the humanity is in and knowing that death is not the end, I tried to stay strong in my centre in this thunder and storms, but I was unwillingly separated from my boyfriend at the moment and my lips... I was so desperate about my bare lips that Corona left without a kiss. More than 4 months I haven't seen him. We did talk on the phone, he is in his 50s, which makes him a non technology person and video talks haven't been our thing. I missed him really much although our relationship was with ups and downs, and separating and uniting frequently, it had been two and a half years almost. I did meet him through a dream and I always felt so loved spiritually, but on the physical realm, we haven't been able to hold on together more than a week, if we stayed together, and when we were far, it prolonged to a month. We never had a normal relation anyway, but I don't remember my lips getting so empty. They didn't get their kiss and had to stay separated from him. Fear of dying when you kiss someone?

But my lips are longing for that kiss the Corona took from me. This kind of fear I wouldn't ever be able to imagine. A fear that stops you from kissing the one you love. It is a fear not just that I will get the virüs. If he gets it because of me and there is the possibility of death. We met in the summer 2020 and it was the strangest return ever – no hugs, no kisses and me as a touchy person was in shock and my boyfriend the whole time was complaining about his hypertension and heart problems. And I was the one denying the dangers of the virüs in the beginning. I did go out meet with people and continued my lessons. And that was for him impossible. So he wanted to protect himself from me. There were so many couples also who didn't care about it and got the Corona together or to some nothing happened. But he was so afraid and I was so afraid that I could cause the illness. What kind of guilt would we have felt if something happened through me? I think this was one of the most challenging things.

Oh my poor bare lips that the corona left without a kiss. In time we did take off our masks and even made love and we even tried with a mask, can you imagine? The most absurd thing… if not a fantasy :) To feel safer – were we dumb? Too cautious? Too scared? When the possibility of death comes, where does the love go? Maybe we were not meant for each other. I don't know. In time we started to get normal, but all these experiences drew us away from each other. Now we are not together anymore!

Life here in Turkey normalised again - the schools are open and the quarantine hours have decreased. Some say it will go back to strict rules again. We'll see! I am still alive and my lips are still longing for the kisses that will be of love and health. What an experience to be on earth in these crazy times..

MARCO, 28 FLORENCE.

Marco Poma - Firenze

March 9, 2020, it's evening, I am in my dark kitchen of the basement house where I live in Florence. It's an ordinary evening spent chatting with, at the time, a new friend and a new partner. Together we watch the news; a new habit, prompted by the growing tension that spreads day by day among the people and which now reaches its peak; the moment we hear the immediate indefinite lockdown announced, something irrevocably changes everyone's lives. For a few months and until this moment, my life took place in the city of the Renaissance, where I moved to do specialist studies in the field of graphic art. I came from Turin looking for new possibilities for my vocation: gradually I was managing to meet my expectations, between new practical skills and social life, and soon I would have ... stop.

I had started a new path and was tackling it with all the energy I knew would allow me to see it accomplished, and now suddenly I find myself ... STOP!

At this moment I feel a vibration shaking my body from below, expanding beyond the confines of a winter crow ... what? Confusion!

In the general frenzy that is unleashed as soon as government directives are disclosed, many off-site young people run for cover, so as not to risk being isolated, for who knows how long, from their families. Among the many, my roommates also decide to return to their respective nests, where they will have the opportunity to spend a more comfortable lockdown. Therefore, they leave space in this house to host other people, so my new friend and my new partner choose to share this "imprisonment" with me.

This new reality turns out to be interesting, the idea of forming a personalised nest with those who, at that moment, represent the ideal company for me in such absurd circumstances, creates in me an intriguing feeling that enriches my sense of loss with new nuances.

You, readers from other places, know well how much Italy is immediately put under pressure by the virus and by the media; so much agitation seems to highlight the apparent calm of a city like Florence. Here, unlike what actually happens in more provincial or even rural areas, the radical change is clearly evident: Florence is a place that, under normal conditions, vibrates and lives on the multitude of people who pervade it and on events. Now it will have to get used to seeing its own deserted streets, while the rows in front of the grocery stores stretch, the balconies are crowded with Italian flags and manifestations of naive positivity: here is therefore improvised patriotism, with applauses of solidarity, national anthems sung to the unison - and, on social media, hashtags of all kinds. The scenario is quite surreal. An invisible enemy makes everyday life disappear, making people themselves invisible, but leaving their fears clearly visible.

What is dystopia in the outside world, seems like a utopia inside, at least initially. The first few weeks become an opportunity to give free rein to the energy and stimuli of being together, almost as if you shared your destiny, and faced it with distraction: at home we cook, watch movies and play. It looks too good to last long. And in fact, it doesn't last, what you learn about living together in quarantine, with someone you basically just met, is that it can go well or drastically bad.

My ego is put under pressure day after day, when I realise that there is no longer a way to distinguish the previous moment from the next. Basically we are in a glass bell, where everything that happens outside is filtered through the four walls of the house.
Inside the glass bell, privacy disappears, relationships tighten and distances are reduced. Cohabitation with my partner proves to be a success: we find the right harmony and create a symbiosis fuelled by good habits, such as cinema, food and afternoon readings - in addition of course to an intense romantic aerobic activity. On the contrary, however, the friend, of an anarchic and introverted disposition, moves further and further away. With her I am unable to carry out a clear and supportive sharing; with her, coexistence ends up ending with a cold hug and the end of a friendship.

Spring, for many - including me - inspires rebirth, thanks to its longer days, milder weather and runaway creativity. For this I bless my little garden, a small green square surrounded by tulips, vines, laurels and bushes with an orange tree dominating the scene. In the shade of this tree I spend every first hour of the day, reading and imagining, helped in concentration by the silence of a city on a break, caressed by the fresh seasonal air and a sweet smell of orange blossoms that remind me with nostalgia at all times of Andalucia.

Faced with this scenario, I live my quarantine. From my bedroom window the garden appears like a painting, free and changing, which reminds me of all the beauty that I am not living out there, but that I am still lucky to be able to see and remember from my green square. So two months pass, fast and intense, and I can't say for sure if the time that passes is similar to the time spent on vacation for me, or if, with a lot of thinking, I'm studying for the return to reality exam. In fact, my reality is not bad and I realise that I have passed the exam when I have the opportunity to return to engraving my works. In fact, it's in the "lockdown" days that I produce one of my best works. Enriched by this stimulus, I realise that my days usually explode with moments that I previously took for granted and that now I see for what they are: ever new opportunities. As often happens, you only realise what you have when you no longer have it.

March 2021, a year has passed. Personally I would not know if the social and health situation in Italy is better or worse than when it started, fortunately none of my loved ones have suffered from this virus. However our freedom is slowly being locked up in what I would now call a social lockdown, where fear and confusion make people suffer and intolerant of everything; I don't know what to think, I don't know who is right or wrong, when in doubt I go on with my life, suffering and rejoicing in silence.

YAZ, 42 DUBAI.

Lock-down!

Life in Dubai was a life lived FAST! It took over and you simply followed its fast and overwhelming track almost uncontrollably. And when it took a toll on you and you had to pause, slow down and take a step back, everyone on that fast track was bombarding you with calls, texts and invites to this fast life. While you apologetically turn them down with a big solid justified excuse, claiming your need to "take it easy, because I have a big busy week ahead" or "I'm sick" or even "I've over done it lately, and I need to slow down". Even such excuses will be followed up by more pressure and it takes a strong will to turn them down.

Yes, this was how it was almost all the time... until... in the distant background a whispered virus started getting mentioned more louder and more often… and it starts visiting closer and closer countries… and leaving a bigger footprint than it was thought it ever would. Then they gave its own unique name. COVID-19. What a silly name we thought. Not knowing that this new C-word will change everything. And I mean EVERYTHING.

It didn't take much time for us to go from work, party, brunch, work, event, supermarket, mall, work, beach, work, boat party, family gathering, work, short weekend getaway, work, birthday weekend, work, ladies night, game night, work ... to WFH, supermarket, FULL STOP. You were home and it was quiet. It alllll calmed down.
The noise, the invites, the convincing, the offers, the "come on, you'll sleep when you die", the "you're becoming a grandpa" - we all were silenced!!
And it felt good! Not only did we stop, but everyone did. And many realised, myself included, that we loved it.
Of course not all did. The lack of distraction, the business trips, short getaways, the events, the parties, the vacations, the camping & fishing trips, lazing by the pool all exposed what was left after you removed all these things. It exposed how much love, substance, truth, acceptance and genuine relationships did one actually have. And that wasn't easy for all.
You had two teams. People that loved this slower pace of life. They enjoyed being home, alone or with loved ones, worked out, discovered new hobbies or simply practiced the things they never had "time" for. People that knew how to make the most out of this 'once-in-a-lifetime experience' and realised that this was a big lesson and life should never go back to that old broken system, but move forward to a more sustainable one. Whilst others were restless, trapped, paranoid, anxious, forced to face their uncomfortable homes, partners and selves...., drank alone more, ordered unnecessary things from Amazon, gained weight, panicked, worked longer and

harder, and simply wanted EVERYTHING to go back EXACTLY how it was ASAP!

How you handled the lockdown was the new measure to differentiate people in Dubai.

NIALL, 31 IRISH IN BALI.

Exactly a year to the day as I write this, my Partner Carla and I were preparing to leave Dublin, Ireland to begin our journey to Bali, Indonesia for our 4th Warriors Retreat of the year.

Our business was up and running, a full year of events coming, we were really excited about getting over to the island of the gods - Bali, a place I once called my second home.

Bali is a magical island and one that I have been visiting for over 13 years. This would have been Carla's first time to visit Bali, and one that she will never forget.

At the time there was a lot of talk in the media and the news regarding the Covid 19 Virus spreading throughout the world, Government advice was not to travel unless it is necessary. Bali was reporting very few cases. So, we decided to go ahead and made the ethical decision to travel as this was our work, little did we know that our days of freedom were numbered.

As we were checking in at the Dublin Airport we met up with Charlotte, who I had known for years and was involved in similar business. She was heading over to Bali for a retreat that she was also facilitating at the same time.

Our plan was to hold the retreat in Canggu where all the activities had been organised.

As the next few days started to unfold my friend Leah who worked in Dubai for Emirates Airlines told me to prepare for the worst and get a flight home to Ireland asap – We decided to stay! But, Carla and I sadly had to confirm that we were calling off the retreat to our participants until further notice.

The main worry we had was that the Government was not releasing any information to the public, any healthcare staff that were caught leaking information or pictures from the inside were to be arrested and sent to jail. The healthcare system was in a state of despair and nobody knew anything creating an immense amount of confusion and panic.

My friend Charlotte joined up with us and we headed for the more peaceful and quiet jungles of Ubud. As the hours went by there were more countries announcing border lockdowns, with all of us glued to our phones we were starting to worry, our embassies were urging all citizens to make arrangements to come back to their home asap or face being stranded. Our insurances companies had also notified us that we would not be insured during this global pandemic.

We decided to get flight home ASAP and spent hours both day and night trying to get flights, only to have them cancelled. Most airports were not allowing non-citizens to transit through domestic into the international airport to get their transiting flight. Operators were still letting you book flights on their system even though there was so much confusion, being stuck in transit or at airports was becoming normality.

Kindly, my brother's friend offered up his holiday villa in Tanahlot, a beautiful oceanside temple area which is one of the most pictured places in Bali. The villa was truly amazing and something you would see in magazines. If there was anywhere you would want to be stuck it was here.

Things started to change really quickly, the local police came to visit us and although they were friendly I felt something wasn't right, Balinese police can be and are well known to be corrupt. They demanded we present our passports, but I refused to give them up, I said that they could take photocopies or pictures, but they cannot hold onto them. We were not allowed to leave the villa and the local community did not like us amongst them.

I was the only one out of all of us that knew the Bali culture, I knew we were in a serious situation if we were not to get out soon. The corrupt justice system in Bali is worrying for westerners. The Government corruption is kept under cover and very little gets leaked for the fear of tourism being damaged, 90% of the economy is driven by tourism.

The Government announced a 14 day lockdown and the first few days looked like the Balinese were enjoying a well-deserved forced holiday, all out and about but very few westerners. This forced holiday enjoyment was not going to last and sooner rather than later I feared we were going to be prime targets for mugging and robberies. I myself had experienced being mugged and robbed over the years in Bali and I know how sophisticated the events take place so I began to worry for all of us.

I sat everyone down this one evening in an urgent request to please follow the instructions, we must not leave the villa, we may be in a beautiful paradise but over the walls every person in the village is watching us, we must trust nobody right now, only ourselves.

We were 3 weeks into Bali lockdown, our time was spent watching the news for new updates or fighting the airlines for refunds for can-

celled flights, we had 22 cancelled flights and our funds were quickly depleting. It was so frustrating and draining so we all decided to just make the most of our time in this Beautiful Villa.
Both Carla and I are coaches in Fitness, Business and Mindset, we would usually have workshops and Retreats in person back home. Carla always had the idea of online coaching so within a day I had Carla's website developed and had online classes and coaching sessions integrated – interacting with her clients which gave a sense of community being so far away.
I got working on my own website and started to book clients in and I was able to make an income. I set my business up to help people in all areas of mindset development, business and fitness.

27 days in Bali now and lockdown is in full force, not being able to go outside the walls of our villa to dip our feet in the sea or relax watching one of mother nature's finest sunsets. The Bali lockdown dream is far from the external representation that our family and friends think we are living…
People that had seen the extent of our worry offered their help – I hold these people in the highest of regards. Great friends don't have to be in contact every day with you, in fact they might be the people you very least expect, they are the ones that offer you help when you don't ask for it but know you may need it.
On day 28 we receive a message from the Irish embassy in Jakarta, there is a repatriation flight that the Portuguese Government is providing to get European Citizens back from Indonesia, and finally

through all this confusion and worry we take the opportunity and part ways with Bali.
As we travel from the Villa to the Airport there is an eerie sense of quietness on the streets, shops which should be thriving with tourists are now nothing but silence. I have much respect for the hard working people of Bali and all the other nations and countries in the world that rely solely on tourism, I definitely think we take things for granted, seeing the bare skeleton of landscape that this pandemic had caused was a sight I will never forget.
Safely home in Dublin I am reminded of all the lessons this year, we have been granted valuable time to grow, learn and develop and we are reminded that there is opportunity to grow everywhere if you are willing to work for it.
It has been a year of undeniable hardship, loss and pain for so many but what I now understand is that we are simply human beings that thrive in environments of good community, healthy balanced nutrition and access to fresh air and exercise –

Everything else in this world is just a blessing and a luxury.

KATALIN, 39 HUNGARY.

After 17 years of being a head designer in a snowboard wear company, then working in films, doing props and set decoration, I decided to leave it all, and follow my heart and become a breath-worker at the age of 39. All this happened because of a magical experience that I encountered thru a breathwork session in a festival in a beautiful valley in Hungary with a group of around 100 people two years ago. That changed my life forever!

I felt so inspired to keep exploring the path of breathwork, that I leased my apartment, so I have enough money to fund my breathwork studies, and so that I can offer free practice sessions for months, and I don't have to worry about finances, while moving thru the phase of becoming an experienced breath-worker. At the end of 2019 I moved back into one of my mother's flats in a more than 100 years old villa, on the top of a hill, located in the centre of Budapest. She was very happy to offer me this help, to host me for a while, especially because we just started to develop a warmer relationship after not really meeting and talking for decades. She really missed me all these years, but whenever we met, I instantly felt triggered by her ways of acting, so I preferred to stay away, to keep the good relationship.

Thru my inner journey in breathwork, I experienced how my frozen relationship with her started to melt, and by the time I moved into the flat over her flat, I actually was really looking forward to being around her, and spend time with her: to finally get to know my mum. She became my number one supporter in my newly found love-job. She listened to my stories about the magic I experienced, and the lessons I learned with such beautiful presence and honest curiosity. She was waiting for me with fresh breakfasts, and delicious lunches between sessions.

Everything was going really beautiful, until at the end of February one of my clients visited Rome for a romantic vacation, and got really sick, and in a week I was also in bed with a really serious flu. For days I couldn't move or eat, and my consciousness was flying somewhere between the sphere of dream world and reality. I had quite serious pains crawling thru my body every second, and I decided, I will fully surrender myself to it, and spend every second by being present to those physical sensations, that shout for attention. This half unconscious state of flow lasted for days, and by the time I was conscious enough again to read news, I found out that Italy went under lockdown to stop the spreading of a fast, and wide spreading virus, that spread to Europe from a Chinese market, where someone ate potentially a bat or a snake.

I found it quite interesting, and started to do a quite deep research on internet about this virus: I was searching for expert interviews, and any studies, that could shine some light on what Italy is facing. I heard in the news, that people are not allowed to leave their flats to slow down the spreading of the virus, and so many people are getting sick, that there is not enough space in hospitals to care about them, and doctors have to choose who to save, and who to let die. We saw private videos of Italian doctors crying in devastation in front of hospitals, not being able to handle the pressure of mass death, and unable to do anything about it. I was still sick, and I remember I started to feel this urge to prepare for the worst. I started to feel this need to share all this to my mum, and also to make some preparations, if this will happen in Hungary also.

I went down to her flat, we had breakfast as usual, and I was trying to share her all the information that I gathered from the internet in the past days, and I advised to do some preparations: start to order food online, wash the hands when entering the flat, and to try to avoid spending time in the middle of crowds, like supermarkets. She reacted to all my suggestions with rejection, and I could feel she finds this all quite ridiculous! She started to tell me how all this is just politics, and then I had to listen to a long angry story about politicians, how they manipulate us... And the story never ended...

So from that moment on, every morning I went down to have that pleasant breakfast with my mum, but we never again talked about our life anymore. I was trying to massage her brain to take care of herself more, and protect herself more, and she was trying to massage my brain to convince me that it's all just politicians messing with us, that the virus is not real, and she was so nervous, and angry. I was still sick, and coughing, having hard time to breath, and I remember that after each conversation with her I felt worse and worse.

She had this feeling around her ideas, that we are all sheep, we are unconsciously driven by politicians, and there is nothing we can do about it. As weeks went by, I started to feel that I am becoming more sick of her ideas, that sneak into my view of reality, than the flu itself. So to keep myself emotionally functional, I decided to set some boundaries, and the next time she started to complain about politicians, I told her, how it makes me feel, and I asked her not to share her fear anymore with me, because it is too much for me. We instantly got into a fight. She got angry and arrogant, talking to me quite aggressive, loud, and telling me, how I disrespect her, and that I shut her up, and don't listen to what she has to say. I told her I can't listen to it anymore.

And there it was, suddenly I found myself in the same shouting and aggressive moment I found myself daily in my childhood... Her face in full expression of sudden hate and anger towards me, and me just feeling this need to run away... just like decades ago. But there was nowhere to run: we were already locked down... I was crying in despair walking up the same stairs I walked up as a child 30 years ago, totally devastated by the attack I received - she telling me, how I am too sensitive, how what I feel is so wrong, how what I am is so wrong... I remember sitting down on the ground in one corner of the room on the carpet, crawling up, hugging myself, and swinging myself like you swing a child to fall asleep... and crying rivers of tears... This desperate cry was so timeless, hours have past, but also for moments I felt like I am still the same child as I was 30 years ago, with the same feelings inside feeling - I am not good enough for my mom, that I will never be good enough. I was in this dreamlike unconscious state crying till the sun went down, sitting in the dark... remembering how I always wanted to kill myself as a child sitting and crying in the same corner, never feeling good enough...

And then suddenly this reassuring, caring sweet inner voice started to get louder and louder saying - you are good enough for me, I love you, and it's ok to cry... And I heard this voice louder and louder, and slowly started to lean my feelings into the caring arms of my inner voice... and that's when I fully went into my deepest darkest hour, feeling fully the feeling of "never being good enough, and being too sensitive"... And then this desperate feeling started to ease, and the part of me holding me safe and caring, and seeing me in pain started to take over, and I suddenly understood It's over. I started to feel, that I get fully anchored into the knowing "I am good enough" and that my sensitivity is a superpower, and not a weakness. I started to feel even gratefulness for being questioned in this deepest way by the person, who can go deepest into my heart. I understood, that after I found my inner voice saying "I am good enough" in front of my mother, there will be no greater authority to be able to destroy this newly found stability...

After all this, I decided not to meet her for weeks. We were in lock-down, not being able to go anywhere. I could hear her talking and coughing, and listening to the news on TV one floor under me, she could hear me walking up and down and coughing one floor over her... but for weeks we didn't talk, just like we haven't talked for decades... Than one day she started to leave some food for breakfast in my kitchen, and we would accidently meet, and she was quite nice, she seemed much softer... and slowly our fear of each other started to melt.

Then one morning she waited for me with some fresh bakery in her hands and a huge kind smile, and she said she doesn't want to lose me again, and looked me in the eye crying... she was so sweet, and all my fear and distancing was instantly melting, and I told her, what I felt: I don't want to lose her again, and we were both crying in relief, bonding into the softest and sweetest hug of my life. This hug felt so honest, and caring, It dried up all the tears of my childhood. We talked, and I understood, that just like she thought I am too sensitive, I thought she is so insensitive. I understood that just like my sensitivity can be superpower, her toughness can also be superpower, I understood that all this two qualities have space in life. We also understood to respect these two qualities, and not try to expect the other to be something else than we are in our true nature... And so that was it... The quarentine that seemed to be my prison for the past weeks, became soft again. We started to embrace the time together: we planted seeds, to grow our own food on our balcony, and started to share what we have in common.

Then after everything settled, I decided to move to our weekend house at a top of an old volcano next to the lake Balaton, the biggest sweet-water lake in Europe. It's a beautiful A frame house in the forest, with an amazing view to the lake. I was there alone all summer, just me and nature. I would only leave for food, and to walk in the forest. People rarely left their houses, so all motor sounds were gone, and for the first time in my life I could finally see this vacation place fully natural, with only sounds of the early summer birds. I felt so free, having no neighbours, I could explore my purest nature. I would wake up before sunrise, dance crazy for my own joy till dawn, then climb the volcano, watch the sunrise from the top, eating all the fresh fruits from the trees of the neighbours on the way back to the garden, then bathing naked in the garden with rainwater in the morning sun and started foraging. Felt like living a dream!

It was a beautiful time as breath-workers started to offer free online sessions, and I would breath every second day, with tens, or hundreds of people from all around the world. As I started to feel more and more free, my expressions grew stronger thru the sessions. As I released my shame, I started to breath naked out under the stars, I would sing out loud, and shout and cry, and touch the ground connecting to mother earth and had magical experiences thru connecting with my own nature, and the nature around me. I made friends around the world online, I learned so much, and really enjoyed the process. I started to feel how I also opened up in the world around me, and by the time I came back to the capital in autumn I was a new person. As we were not allowed to leave the house after 8.00 p.m. and no public places were open to gather, people started to have their social life in homes, which was not so common before. People started only invite people they are really willing to share time with. Soon I found myself to be part of women circles, singing circles, I started rock climbing with these groups.

After all, I have to say, that 2020 was probably one of the most magical years of my life. Thanks to it, everything that didn't serve me, just left me, and right now I am so grateful for the life I live, enjoying every day the ups and the downs, with the understanding that they all serve us in one way or the other. And, I feel this joy of looking forward to the rest of my life, living it fully, exploring how it feels to live a life where I am good enough every day as I naturally am.

SAVITA, 33, GERMAN IN BERLIN/CENTRAL AMERICA

The first lockdown hit at the best possible time. And the worst possible time. The best in hindsight. It's always in hindsight, that we manage to see those silver linings. While being in it - there is nothing to see, nothing but fog and dark clouds, snowstorms and heavy rains. Literally. Because the first lockdown I spend in the grey, wintery Berlin.

It was the worst possible time, because I had just walked out of an eight year relationship. A relationship? The relationship. The man of my life, the one I married, ran wild with. The one that taught me how to ride a motorcycle, that took me travelling, that cared for me and protected me. I had walked away from a whole life, full of adventure and friends and plans and love.

And now I sat in an empty room, alone, in a city I barely knew. Frail, shakily trying to somehow reinvent myself, or at the very minimum make some sense of myself. Every plan I ever laid out wiped away. That was February. The Corona news trickling in from China barely on the periphery of my vision.

The little 2-bedroom I was living in was left sticky with dirt by the previous tenants. There were half rotten jars piling in the fridge, the sink leaking, my clothes half moulded in plastic bags in the cellar.
I didn't know many people in the city and the few I did were friends of my husband. I barely ever called anyone. Instead, I bought bottles of wine from the kiosks on the street, laid on the couch and opened up my tinder when half-drunk at night. I started meeting men and women in the bars, but hardly ever taking them home. Once I asked someone to leave mid-sex.
Nothing seemed to make any sense at all.
The last party: I was laughing at people in the queue, that were afraid of catching the virus. That night, I got so high, the friends I came with left me angrily, "You can't expect other people to take care of you all the time." So I stayed back, fucked a girl in the dark on the side of the dance floor, did lines in a random Ikea-furnished apartment until late in the afternoon on the following day.
After that weekend I got sick and stayed sick for three weeks. I don't know if it was Corona, an infection, or just my body revolting. I barely had the energy to make it down to the supermarket - eating whatever was left in some of the cans the previous tenants left, barely moving from the bed. When I finally got better, the lockdown started and my grandmother passed away and I had not gone to see her to say goodbye. I was walking through the empty grey streets like a dream. Something in me relaxed because suddenly the world around

me seemed just as lost in the gap as I was. Something in me tensed because I knew there was nowhere to go for me now, nothing to discover, nothing to plan, nothing to distract me.

The months were a blur. There were good days, trying to wake up early, forcing myself down the stairs and into the little park around the corner. There were some zoom-calls, work appointments. There were a lot of black days. Days that I started with red wine and just continued with it, waiting for me to be able to get back to sleep, just to wake up in the middle of the night and stare onto my cell-phone screen until the morning. There were days that I enjoyed this. There were many more in which I hated myself to my guts. I read books about white privilege and hated myself. I read self-help books and hated myself for not being able to help myself. I read about self-hate and hated myself for hating myself.

Fast forward to February 2021. The border between Honduras and El Salvador. My hair is military short, only a small Mowhawk running through the center of my head. My shoulders are dark brown, the days heat is pulsing through my body and blood, while I am smiling and bantering with a fat lady selling nuts and cigarettes. I still feel the taste of the last night somewhere in my sweat. There is a melody in my steps, a rhythm even though my thighs hurt, and I don't know if it's from sex or from riding a horse bare-backed a few days ago. I have no plans and don't care to have any. I carry my tiny backpack across one shoulder and under the bright sun everything seems possible, as I pass my passport and the black and white printout of a Covid test through the little counter window to the border patrol, grinning wide under the covers of a shabby facemask.

What had happened? Where was the woman with the dark shades under her eyes, crawling drunkenly on the carpet in her Berlin apartment, looking for a Xanax she had dropped under the couch?

The first thing that woman had to learn was to cry. And I remember it took me two months to begin to learn it. She had to wait until she really truly had enough. Enough of busying herself, with shitty graphic-jobs, amazon orders, endless Netflix series, red-wine. Enough of lying in bed and staring at the ceiling.

I remember that one morning, I decided to feel - the dark hole, the shitty piercing pain that was sitting in my chest ever since I had walked away from the man I married. I had ignored it, drugged it, busied myself, I had spited it and avoided it. But I hadn't felt it. But there, in the four walls of a single room, in the middle of lockdown - there was no way to run away from it.

So I sat crying. It lasted the whole day. And the next one. It was scary to cry like this, it felt like once I started it would never stop. But I kept going. Right there into that pain, aching like a physical injury in the middle of my chest, this sweetest rawest part of me that no one, but my man had ever touched. The loss of that comfort, the warm skin I had cuddled up against for most of my adult life. The familiar smell. The silly laughs in the early mornings. The children we had wanted. The way his voice turned sweet and his face turned soft, when we talked about them. And in between the tears, waves and waves of fear rolling in. How could I possibly make it on my own, in that world that is so big, and sometimes cruel, scary and loud, and now completely changed, by this strange virus? Who could I possibly be, alone?

Lying there shaking and crying on the carpet, after some hours I found out that I was able hold myself. That I could physically wrap my arms tight around my body, like a friend. Like a lover. And that the waves of fear and sadness would pass through me, when I held myself like that.

When I didn't cry, I sat quietly on the couch. I had been to many meditation retreats, but now I wasn't trying to meditate. My mind was just quiet, there were no words, I just sat, resting, letting breath move in and out, not waiting. Not doing anything. Until more tears would come, and I would hold me again, and let them come.

And somehow from there things began making sense.

I cleaned out the cellar, I threw away most of my clothes. I forced myself to go to a few yoga classes out in the park, panting and sweating through the one and a half hours. I forced myself to cook meals, even though I could barely finish them. And I made a decision. I was going to learn how to love myself. There was pretty much no other choice. There was no way I could go on like this and no distraction, no job, no book was going to help me. And nothing that I would attempt doing, could possibly be of any worth, as long as I wasn't able to be my own friend.

As the summer came I spend more time outside. I went to visit friends on a Greek island. I went to mediation and yoga classes, first weekly, then daily. Whenever I felt tired, hopeless, helpless, I squeezed my arms tight around my chest, to remind myself.

As the world was figuring out, what to do in this strange new situation, so was I. For a while, life seemed almost normal. The parks were full of people. I made some new friends. I slept with a few men.

Then October came. With the first nights of the icy winter rains, the news started trickling in again, the schools closing, the curfews, the constant repetition of case numbers. And this time I was prepared. Or at least prepared to be absolutely unprepared. Few countries still had open borders. Africa, Central America. Eastern Europe. I didn't wait long. The day they introduced the curfew, I bought a ticket to Panama City. I had never been to Central America, I had never heard anything about the country – they had hats and a canal, apparently. For all I knew.

It did not matter. I would not sit enclosed in the four walls of that same apartment. I would not walk the wintery empty streets again, circling the same pathways through my neighbourhood. I had healed a bit and I had learned. To hug myself tight when I was afraid. And to cry when I was sad. What else would I need?

I packed a tiny backpack, hand-luggage only. A few shirts, pants, underwear. And made it to the airport early in the morning, the subways already eerily empty again.

From here on I don't have a lockdown story to tell. I refused to get locked down. I used the privilege I had, my Central European passport, my small funds and the biggest privilege of all - having a friend travelling with me. Always. Resting in my own two arms, that were ready to give me a hug whenever I needed one.

The rest of my Covid story is full of wonders. Fairy tale nights in the Nicaraguan jungles. Giant Tarantulas, butterflies, howler monkeys. Sleeping in El Salvadorian hostels. Getting my credit card stolen on a border crossing. Swimming in the Caribbean Ocean. Learning Spanish. Drinking Rum, playing snooker, doing cocaine with the local surfer guys. Dancing in dingy bars. Buying myself a second-hand dirt bike and riding it up and down the coastline. The rest of my Covid story is not a Covid story at all. I am sitting in a hostel in Tulum writing this, no part of me even considers to return to Europe any time soon. I chose to be free, and I am still choosing to be free. I'm dreaming of opening up a hostel in Nicaragua. Or teaching Meditation in Tulum. Or working on a sailboat to criss-cross the Caribbean islands. But I know it does not matter that much. I made a choice, somewhere all the way back almost a year ago, on a wine stained carpet. To be my friend.

I might have found this out without the help of a global pandemic. I might not have. But I walk gratefully, because for whatever reason it happened, the only thing that counts is that it did.

I learned that I have a **choice.**

KIRSTY, GLASTONBURY UK.

A message from Avalon, Glastonbury. Also known as, the heart centre of the earth. Famous for the Glastonbury Festival, but the little town itself has long been a place of spiritual pilgrimage. Connected to the legends of Merlin and even more the travels of Mary Magdalene. The divine feminine resides here. The energy and magic of this land has not stopped throughout the lockdown, the drumming and dancing on the Tor under the light of the full moon has continued throughout. It has been a shining light and place of hope. As the heart centre, Avalon is a microcosm of the whole planet.

Part way through the first lockdown a dear friend had travelled to Glastonbury in his van, on his return he showed us pictures of the beautiful land and told us stories of the community thriving. My whole heart exploded, with a big fat YES, that is where I need to go. So, me and my partner packed up our stuff within the next month and left the city of Brighton, to Somerset. It turned our whole lives upside down, but with the lockdown already doing that, there was no doubt for either of us that this was right. Leaving Brighton was a breath of fresh air and a sense of relief.

As soon as we arrived in Glastonbury, my whole being relaxed, this is what I now know as a common feeling for one entering the town. It is what I call receiving a hug from the Goddess. After a month of living in a tent together under the Tor, me and my partner parted ways, it was painful, but right. If you aren't sure that everything happens for a reason, come to Glastonbury for a while.

It is more obvious here than anywhere else I have been - it doesn't take much to notice the intricately woven threads of our life and how we are being led. Every time I walk down the high street serendipity happens, the right place at the right time with the right people, it becomes clear none of it is an accident. With some grief of a relationship ending, I chose to count my blessings and continued counting them. I had come to settle in a place where there is a real community, a fully supporting network of sisterhood. A place with the blessing of spiritual elders to share their wisdom, and a blossoming relationship with the trees, plants, hills and land. These are the things that have kept me anchored.

What happens a short while after the uplifting sense of peace on arrival, has been called "The Glastonbury Experience". A process of death and rebirth begins. Not physical death, this death happens in the unseen realms of our psyche and internal world. It is a shedding of layers, like a snake sheds its skin. It is the death of everything that is no longer the truth of our spirit. Imagine a snake keeping on its old skin, and when it grew a new layer it kept that skin on too, and so on, and so on… Eventually, the snake would be trapped, suffocated by that which is dead and should have been let go of long ago. Possibly, it would forget that there is another way, that it does not have to carry all its old, dead skin and in the end, it might even die, long before its time, thinking that was all it had left.

These past months I have been that snake. It's tested my bravery, ability to self-enquire, trust in love and my willingness to change. Now, I am beginning to remember the freedom of fresh scales. Collectively we are all that snake, and as a human race, we have just started shedding, beginning with the pandemic being the biggest upheaval of our lives as a collective in our known history.

At moments this process of shedding and remembering is like the freedom and beauty of first entering Avalon, and sometimes it is painful and confusing as we unravel the old. So, this is the message for all of us right now. Just as the red and white springs of Avalon continue flowing, and the drummers on the Tor continue drumming, there is always a place where the richness of life flows, it is found in the heart. There are forces at work beyond our awareness, and coming together in community to hold each other through the difficult times, we can become more alive than ever.

SHIRA, 32 ISRAEL.

Yesterday me, my husband, my 4 year old boy and my 2 year old girl, went to visit our expanded family After we did not see them almost six months.

You see, Corona turned all our lives upside down. And in August 2020, me, and my husband, after 7 years of living in the big city, we decided to leave to someplace quieter.

The city's rough energy was "strangling" us, it seemed to us like the over population and stress of the people living in the city made everyday life chaotic for us. Every going out for groceries is like entering a battle zone, every person you come across is a potential enemy.

Here in Israel, the media who is controlled by the government, decided to abuse the term "mutual responsibility" and to appoint the citizens to be each other's law enforcement. They encourage us to rat out on each other with the help of a national "hotline" where you can anonymously complain if your neighbour is "overcrowding" or not wearing mask. Television commercials encourage people to demand from other people around them to immediately wear a mask, in the name of our health.

Because the craziness just kept growing, we found a house far from the city and completely turned our life around to stay away from everything Corona related.

Our children started an alternative "forest kindergarten" who works "under the radar" and does not follow quarantine orders

We surrounded ourselves with friends who think and feel like us, and together we support each other. We permanently closed the TV and stopped listening to the harsh, dividing, constant propaganda.

And everything was fine. We stayed strong and resilient to the often quarantine, who was absolutely detached from reality. We stood against the sanctions and the pressure against the Israeli population to get the untested unsafe "vaccine", and all the corona saga became nothing but an interesting dinner talk.

That is until yesterday.

The day we went to visit our expanded family, I'm talking about people who live and breathe TV news channels, eating fear for breakfast , all of them unexceptionally, received willingly 2 shots of vaccination to "protect" themselves and others.

They don't ask questions they don't get angry when the government plays with us like puppets and refer to themselves proudly as: "obedient".

As soon as we walked through that door, the magnitude of the plague just hit us with full force. Everybody is covered in masks (inside the house!), 2 meters of social distancing between each other, And of course when the "unvaccinated" family came in, 2 meters became 4, and we were even explained that two of our cousins who are currently serving in IDF, got specific orders from their commanders to stay away from unvaccinated people, so please don't come any closer.

At that moment, a realization hit me that life in Israel got split into two different realities.

Once the Corona circus started, two different dimensions and mindsets were opened and it created a situation, that 2 people who stood next to each other, they could even be husband and wife, or blood related and each one of them lives in a completely different world.

Corona emphasized the difference between our minds and created for each person a complex physical world costume made just for him.

One, fell into a scary intimidating world, a world with a deadly virus who kills healthy people, and for our protection and safety, we are stripped out of our human rights, and so bad and so unjust, that it reminds us of past darker days, of Nazis and holocaust.

And the other one, moved to live in a world of faith, a world where love is first, love exists and reveals itself to us every single day. A Godly world. Where you wake up in the morning thankful for this day, and everything in it. In this world you learn how to miss a heartbeat over a beautiful flower, you learn what are your strong and weak points, you get to know yourself, and why you are here. It is a complicated exciting beautiful world, and its more real than ever.

So, you see my friends, that's why if you ask me "what is going on in Israel", the pool of answers is never-ending.

And all of it is true.

The pressure that is being pressed on Israelis is huge like a steam roller.

We are an experimental state.

There are vaccination stands outside of shopping malls and parks And we are not allowed to get in if we did not get a shot and have a certificate to prove it.

They plunder the vaccinated population against people who refuse to get the vaccine. They use the television and the news to tell the people that unvaccinated people are dangerous, they spread the virus. They are the reason our life stopped, they are the reason we go into quarantine every month, because of them old people die and young kids don't go to school and get education.

They closed us in our homes saying, "it will stop the virus" closed businesses all over the country, citizens lost all their money, they can't pay their mortgage anymore, and a lot of them struggle to put food on the table.

And in all that chaos, a little seed of new understanding is growing

We start to realize, that human beings are very strong and resilient, we have the power and the ability to change and to adapt ourselves into new situations, IF WE ONLY CHOOSE TO.

If we could only take back the responsibility to ourselves, the simple truth will become clear there is nothing outside of us who has the power to enslave us, to tyrannize us, or force us.

The responsibility and blame are not on the government, not on Bibi Netanyahu or in the fake-news room.

The responsibility is in each and everyone of us who consciously or unconsciously choose every moment of every day, to throw the responsibility away from him, or to take it and be a proud creator of his own story.

When you put the blame of the circumstances of your life on other people you put YOURSELF in a prison of suffering and fear.

I believe it is not a coincidence I won the privilege of writing this today and that's why as I'm sitting in my home, the sunshine fills the room through the open window

the only answer I can think of to the complicated question: "what is going on in Israel these days?!" is: "SOMETHING BIG"

With Special Thanks

KAY, 63, UK CITIZEN RESIDING IN PERU.

For several weeks I had been trying to find the words to tell my partner that I no longer wanted to remain in our shared business, and to move away from the city. I had tried a couple of times, but failed to find the right words... Right words being ones he would understand as real, here and now, rather than some part of a distant, unknown but vaguely planned future, where we would finish building the house we had started in the mountains.

The business was a rocking success, our first - personal and passionate in that everything was hand-made; and represented four years of consistent work. It was also the plan for how we would finance the house. No wonder I wasn't finding the words, but suddenly they were taken right out of my mouth, as we watched what appeared originally to be a lab leak in China turn into a "pandemic". The reports from China disappeared rapidly as politicians tried to silence "conspiracy theorists" and the media filled and overflowed with hype about the virus and the lockdown rules. Then the day arrived -16th March 2020. Full lockdown in Peru.

We sat and discussed how we would deal with being locked in the house (rented, flat, square, cement, ground floor only, small central patio, no garden, no view) the two of us and our special son. We decided that the most important things would be communication and space, and that we would deal with any issue that came up as it came up and never leave anything unsaid. We recognised it would be a test for the relationship, and quietly, hopefully, in a chrysalis inside me a subtle change took place, as I redefined it as a test for our projected life in the mountains, and I secretly began to wonder if the pandemic was going to be my best friend.

The business - an arts and crafts shop in a very successful tourist centre not far from Lima was booming and open as usual until the day before lockdown began. At home, with our son, I pictured my partner in the shop and thought of the passing of coins and shaking of hands with all those tourists, and wondered if I believed the hype about hand washing and alcohol. I had internally debated a suggested idea of using magic to seal our house against this "invisible enemy that could live on anything and infect by touch".

My son has febrile epilepsy and as flesh eating, fear mongering, media-fed weevils tried to nest in my mind, my inner voice kept saying "whatever it is, it's here... make peace with it, you need immunity not denial." Sure enough in the first days of lockdown we all brewed up high temperatures, burning throats and compulsive coughs. I spun into action with home remedies: infusions, essential oils, gargles, inhalations, mouthwashes on a regimented schedule, and of course paracetamol to lower temperatures. Within 3 days we were all recovering. I don't know if it was Covid, but whatever it was, we all made peace with fear, and I was reminded that I know how to deal with viruses. I'm grateful for that.

We settled into living in confinement, and began to enjoy our commitment to communicate and give space. Respect for each other under duress. We fell more deeply in love, and 3 days later my partner asked, "So if we move to the mountains, we can live like this all the time and not have to run schedules, keep paperwork and toil our arses off?" - "Yes", I said, with that little chrysalis of hope beginning to prepare butterfly wings in my heart. He stared with wide thoughtful eyes for a few moments and declared, "Ok we're closing the business to move to the mountains

That was the early delight of lockdown: the trials began soon after, as our landlady moved into the vacant flat upstairs, from where she could see and hear our patio through her bedroom window. Regularly observed, and now struggling to uphold our agreement about communication for distaste at being overheard, we became quieter, withdrawn, our son got ill. Navigating the health system here is not easy at the best of times. Under lockdown it was a nightmare. But the butterfly of hope continued gestating.

The television news became more real - instead of so many reports about Covid statistics, in a country that has no benefits system and a massive unregistered economy, we began hearing the true stories about how people were facing hardship. Stories of collaboration and heroism: communities were creating Covid kitchens. In Lima the "oxygen king" was trying to ensure that there was an alternative to the sharks who were charging blood and flesh for breath.

Stories of desperation and heroism: the street sellers in the city, who had arrived thinking the streets were paved with gold, now finding themselves suddenly banned from their avenues of economy and with nothing to eat, facing police and soldiers. Covid lifted the curtains on a mounting, consuming, tidal wave of poverty, and many of those brave adventurers who had left the rainforest, mountains, pampa to make a "better life", that would enable them to send financial support to their families, began to realise that the only way was back.

And so began their long walk home. I don't know how many tears of disbelief I shed watching the footage of caravans of people walking 3 days, 7 days, more... and arriving to hostile communities, who feared them as lepers because they were coming from the city, and made them quarantine outside before being allowed back into their own lands and houses. Tears of disbelief that they had to do it, tears of relief as the stories of people making it home reached the news, tears of humility in the face of human fortitude.

For me now, the butterfly was on the wing. We weren't to walk it, we would be able to load our stuff onto a lorry and get to our place in a couple of days as soon as travel restrictions were lifted, because I'm a gringa and have a credit card. That Ìs true privilege in a pandemic.

By August the rules were eased. We mothballed the shop and began the process of packing, all the time thinking that we would leave our son with his aunty, whilst we made the house in the mountains habitable. Up to now, it had walls and a roof – no windows, doors, electricity or water supply, and the thought of trying to install all that at the same time as caring for a special child seemed much more scary than the thought of Covid had been. Then the blockages started - things going wrong, breaking, finding ourselves unable to make decisions, losing contacts....... until we finally got the message that we should all go together. We checked with the driver whether it would be ok to take our son in the cab, and with confirmation that we could, things began to flow.

The journey itself was difficult - There were police stops requiring "tips". The wind was against us. The first lorry broke down and we had to hire another. I lost the cats. I had figured they would cope with 2 days, and they did, but as we were reloading the second lorry, I debated with myself whether they would make it. I was ready to persuade the cafe owner in the truck stop to take them, but the new driver assured me we would arrive that evening, and I figured they would be ok. We didn't arrive that evening, we had to stop again overnight, and at some point they escaped. I'm glad they escaped and I didn't find them dead. Lessons in survival and the fortitude of the feline spirit.

On arrival we quarantined in the house at it was - boarded up with plywood in the windows, and with 2 doorways stuffed with foam mattresses. The ground floor was still basically damp rubble waiting for cement, but we had one room downstairs that we could cordon off and turn into sleeping space, and there we all huddled for the first 2 weeks, sleeping in our clothes underneath mountains of blankets. I won't go into detail suffice it to say I have concluded that after about 10 days bodies become self-cleaning.

At this point, the second floor didn't have a balcony or staircase. The joists were in place to build the balcony and we had floorboards laid loose on top. Once out of quarantine we got the windows put in and raised a ladder to the wobbly boards, and, with his 14 year old son on his back, my partner began each night to climb the ladder, walk the planks, and get in through a window, while I stood by to "help" if necessary, with my heart in my mouth.

Sleeping upstairs enabled us to begin work on the ground floor, and since then we have gradually been able to open the house to the beauty of its surroundings, and fill it with light. We now have doors, a balcony with stairs our son can manage, built by a local craftsman, and we're in the process of installing a brick built, wood fired oven/hob/stove with a water tank that, in tandem with solar hot-water panels will feed our hot water system. When we get solar electricity and a ground water pump, we should be able to go off-grid, but for now, we have water and electricity supplies "borrowed" from an empty house next door, and a vision of where we are going.

I love living this indoor-outdoor mountain life and integrating myself into a community that lives hand in hand with Mother Earth. A self-governing community that holds regular council meetings, which (among other things) are used to organise maintenance of the tracks (there aren't any "made" roads) and waterways. At times of seeding and harvest they practice Ayni (everyone works everyone else's field, and the host provides food and drink for the day of labour; that way everyone has a task force at minimal cost, and the work is turned into a sharing party) People here are wise, innocent and happy. They always smile and greet as they pass, and often stop to ask how things are going.

Although the time of Lockdown in Lima was difficult, I'm eternally grateful for it because it provided the impetus to get us away from commerce and the city. Whatever the world holds for us next, I begin from a place of peace and creativity, catapulted by a pandemic to take authority over my own existence and activate my dream. I wish the same for everyone, especially for those people who had to make the long walk home. I wish that humanity will come to recognise that the Inca were right – real abundance is to be found in the gold of the corn, not paving city streets. Here, in the simplicity of this community, I always step out with a little bubble in my chest wondering what conversations I'm going to have today, and what animals, insects and plants I will find. One thing I know for sure is that a butterfly will always cross my path, glittering its dance of hope in the mountain sun.

JONATHON, 51 COSTA RICA/EQUADOR.

Green Leaves Sprout After the Yellow Ones Have Fallen By: Jonathon Miller Weisberger

"Your task is not to seek for love, but merely to seek and find all the barriers within yourself that you have built against it." ~ Rumi

The universe is a holograph and everything is reflected inside everything, from the smallest to the largest, from the remotest past to the most distant future, and each person's story is an inseparable part of the collective story of humanity. Each soul is dancing in the ebb and flow of an eternal sacred unfolding universe. The only constant being change. Stories help us understand the vital importance of experiencing this unity and riding the waves of change. Imparting at the very least entertainment and at the most vital guidance towards clarifying each person's "filters" Allowing people to see the importance of releasing ideologies, shaking off superficial opinions and learning the deeper truth that help us see what can be accepted, all the while imparting the wisdom to know what it is that we can actually change. What it is we can reform, and what can be transformed! Stories guide us in the painful and yet utterly beautiful path of surrendering to love and to learning to see the reality of life. So that we may see life for what it simply is. This way, no matter what happens, at the very least, one's spirits may always be free. To me this is the purpose of all great stories.

And while the world is in lockdown, somewhere over hills and fields ...

An eagle...

circle's around,

over a green valley,

through a clear blue sky, ...under a golden yellow sun.

My partner Moni was pregnant, she was in Ecuador where she's from. I was raised in Ecuador, a country I know well. Since the year 2000 we've lived together most of the year on the Osa Peninsula, in Costa Rica, at our family run nature lodge, the Ocean Forest Ecolodge - also known as Guaria de Osa. I had just finished attending to yet another all-time epic Rainforest Medicine Council Gathering with a collective of beautiful souls. This was December 2019. January 2020 came around and despite it being my most absolutely favourite time of the year on the Osa Peninsula, I was soon to leave for Equador. The rainy season had past and upon us has come the onset of the dry season. The yage vines were flowering prolifically. Fresh ocean breezes clean the shores and the forest shines as the birds and animals all evidently share in their delight. No more dumping rains, nor large trees falling over, for the time being that is, and the cicadas are shrilling from the treetops. A beautiful collective of allies – were there to help run the lodge, and the time came for me to leave. My first child was due to be born any day, and off I left, without looking back, for the airport towards Ecuador.

Arriving to Ecuador late January 2020, Monica looked so good, large round belly, rosy cheeks and happy as can be to see me and to be expecting our first child. Not but a week later I was painting a flower of life mandala on her belly, and then, as if all the months of anticipation suddenly whirled into a flashing moment, baby slipped through into the here and now, from the deepest inner mystery into this present reality. There with my two hands on Monica, channelling Reiki, at noon mid-day on the 28th of January, amidst a group of loving souls experienced in facilitating babies being born, a gorgeous and healthy baby girl arrived.
Those first few nights after her birth I received some powerful dreams. A mysterious crescent moon hung low over the mountain of Pichincha that night of her first day in this world, and remarkably so, just under the moon, Venus was shining like we had never seen before.

We were planning to head back to the lodge in Costa Rica a few months after baby was born. When most suddenly, and unexpectedly with no advance notice, BOOM, lockdown! The airports were closed, interprovincial transport closed, the entire situation just over night was made present for the whole world to see!

Suddenly I had a whole lot of time, in a small apartment in a bustling popular neighbourhood of El Inca, smack in the middle of Ecuador's capitol city. Quito means the beginning and it is one of the oldest continually inhabited cities in America, and given all the people that live here, people seem to find their way along. A quality characteristic of old places, where people have been through all kinds of experiences and all kinds of suffering. Ecuador is a land of stark contrasts. High mountains and low valleys, deserts and rain drenched forests. And here I find myself in a place I never really thought I'd find myself in. Not a single tourist around here that's for sure. Lots of street vendors, and all kinds of food for exaggeratedly low prices, makes you realize economies are based on what the local people can afford, at least around here. Thank goodness despite the lock down, here the food never went scarce. Our local shops loaded with all types of fruits, grains and vegetables. And it is heart-warming yet tragic to see regular people sharing the little they have with the Venezuelan immigrant families wandering the streets with babies, seeking ways to start anew. Ecuador is a land of contradictions – everything is what it seems and is not what it seems at the same time. A land where the poor eat the good food they grow, and the financially more affluent eat the overpriced junk food from the modern supermarkets. A place where who you think will the biggest butthole can be your best ally, where magic happens and everything is just dangling in the open.

I once heard a story imparted to me by my good-hearted friend and ceremonial guide, Cesareo Piaguaje traditional elder of the Siekopai people. His grandfather, Yai JoseÌ Piaguaje had a prophetic vision during a ceremony of yage at the wilderness lagoons of Peë'quë'yá, the Black Caiman Lakes, located on the edge of what today is the boundary between Ecuador and Peru - at the heart of the Siekopai people's ancestral homelands. Yai JoseÌ, Cesareo related, saw that a time would come when Kenovi, the beast of the apocalypse, would be slain and yanked from inside the earth. Kenovi is believed to be the source of all world chaos. The slain beast would be brought all over the world. It would be carried over the entire planet by divine immortals exhibiting it in plain daylight for everyone to see. Only their hands, the people of the earth would see, holding the annihilated monster, chains hanging from its drooping dead body. Following would come a time of peace and prosperity to all humanity.

"And how shall you rise beyond your days and nights unless you break the chains which you at the dawn of your understanding have fastened around your noon hour?" – Khalil Gibran

And so I found myself tackling some really heavy scenarios. Daily working to shed bitterness, shedding of resentment, shedding fear, peeling away the layers, peeling away the chaos inside of me brought on by the entire scenario of the world and us in lockdown, and all the related implications. Feeling and seeing the hardships and sorrow people are undergoing, and experiencing some of this myself, brought Rumi's words echoing their blessed truth:

"Sorrow prepares you for joy. It violently sweeps everything out of your house, so that new joy can find space to enter. It shakes the yellow leaves from the bough of your heart, so that fresh, green leaves can grow in their place. It pulls up the rotten roots, so that new roots hidden beneath have room to grow. Whatever sorrow shakes from your heart, far better things will take their place."

And I found myself, nurturing our newborn baby, a precious innocent life. And working diligently to keep my family business afloat, and to uphold the living breathing universal culture of service. And I can say, with joy and gratitude, while the state of the world dangles in a precarious place, I have chosen the path of love over the path of fear. And in my heart, the yellow leaves have blown away and green leaves have sprouted.

JESS, 41 LONDON/READING.

If someone had told me that in the not-so-distant future, the whole world would be locked down with businesses and all childcare, including schools closed - I'd have laughed in their face. Prior to lockdown my little girl, Namaya was at her childminders Monday to Friday, leaving me with ample time to work on my growing business. I loved living in London, it was my home for 14 years and, to be honest, I couldn't see myself ever wanting to leave. The choice of things to do, everything at a convenient reach 24/7 kept me wanting to be there.

However the reality was, I didn't get to spend enough quality time with Namaya. When she came home at 6.30 and then it was time for bed two hours later. I felt sad that I wasn't with her during the day and had missed so many firsts. At times I felt the guilt of having to be away from her most of the days of the week. As a single mother, I was the provider for her - the roof over our heads, the clothes on our back, and the food in our tummies. On top of that, we were living in a tiny flat in Camden with no outside space, blocks of flats on either side with screaming families to boot. I saw nothing but concrete out the windows. It was far from ideal.

In 2018 I realised I didn't want Namaya to grow up in Camden, the gang crime with young kids is insane! The thought of her getting caught up with that made me realise I would have to move before she hit school age, but where would I go? All I kept thinking of was that I wanted to be somewhere surrounded by grass and trees.

When lockdown hit it was a shock to the system, how would I manage a day's work around Namaya? How would this impact her? Would I be able to cope?

The first few weeks were tough. It was hot, my small flat used to reach some crazy temperatures when it was warm outside and I was trying to sneak work in here and there. I tried to figure out a system where I could attend to Namaya's needs and the needs of my business. I resigned myself to the fact that I'd have to free myself as much as possible during the day and then catch up on anything work-related in the evening. I did the same system when she was a baby of few months old and onwards (until childcare came about) but back then without a team to help me, sometimes I'd be up working until 2 am.

I felt bad for my little girl, whilst she was happy to be spending time with me, I realised the lockdown wasn't going anywhere, anytime soon. I felt living in such a small space would eventually have a negative impact on her, especially if the weather wasn't great and we had to stay in.

Luckily for the first part of lockdown, the weather was amazing and we weren't too far from Hampstead Heath, so we could escape the flat daily to get some outside time. But getting out the door with kids is never quick and easy! It was at least an hour event to make it out the door, with a guaranteed 'I need a poo' just as we were about to set foot over the threshold. I thought how amazing it would be to simply open my door and see her run outside into a garden.

A second wave was already being talked about before the first lockdown had even ended. I knew I had to make my escape when the restrictions eased off and I knew London was well and truly off the menu. Everything that made London fun was gone and I couldn't deal with another flat. I started to realise how important it was going to be to connect to nature as much as possible during this process. So with this in mind, I went online to search.

I found the perfect place immediately; it was literally the first house that popped up after I searched and I knew that was the place for us. I could totally imagine living there complete with a veggie patch and dog. Not only was it surrounded by more grass and trees than I could ever have imagined, but it was also inside a botanical garden. Let me tell you I have never worked so hard on manifesting something in my whole entire life. All I thought about was the house. Every spare second I had I was imagining myself being there with Namaya, us running around and playing in the garden. I convinced myself so much that the house was mine that at one point I nearly started packing! I wanted this for us so badly, I knew it would be a game-changer.

My 40th birthday was spent 95% alone as my daughter was with her father. The night before my birthday my phone broke so I knew I wouldn't be able to have calls on the day! I had huge plans for my 40th, which obviously went tits up with the lockdown, but I couldn't feel sad about it. I knew if I was alone and totally uninterrupted then I could focus all my energy on manifesting the house.

Two days later, after waiting for two weeks I got a call from the estate agents, they told me out of all of the people who'd applied to live there, they'd chosen us! I was at Hampstead Heath at the time with Namaya and I literally started jumping up and down with joy. We were so excited! But then around a week later I started to have a freak-out. I was about to leave London, my home for the last 14 years, where all my friends were and my three sisters lived - to move to a place further south, where I didn't know anyone, even further away from my parents in Newcastle. On top of that, because of the restrictions I hadn't even viewed the property, I wouldn't be able to until the old tenants had moved out, which turned out to be 6 days before I moved in!

The thing is, it's normal to get doubts creeping in whenever we're about to embark on a new journey; it's the ego's way of protecting us from making mistakes and keeping us out of harm's way. But it can also massively block us! I started to recall all the times I had moved to a new area where I didn't know anyone and it all turned out great! This would be the fourth time that I have done this, so why was I so scared?

I reminded myself I was a short train ride back into London should I want to go and visit. I knew this house was a once-in-a-lifetime chance, it was quirky and I could really see myself happy there, and most importantly feeling the freedom I was lacking confined to a shoebox. I got over this quickly and went back to feeling super excit-ed.

Once I moved in I was able to completely submerse myself in the surroundings and I immediately knew I'd made the right decision. For me, if I'm that excited about something in the beginning, it always turns out to be the right thing to do. Doubt can creep in, but that doesn't mean it's not for you! For the first time in my life, I felt like I had a work-life balance.

Because lockdown ended childcare, and I wasn't able to work during the day, I was now in a place where I could really enjoy the time more.

Even though it's brought about a lot of change and challenges, if it wasn't for lockdown I would still probably be where I was before. I mean I would have moved at some point, but this really gave me a kick up the backside that I didn't even know I needed! This experience has put everything into perspective and made me understand on a deep level what actually is really important to me, what really matters in my life. Sometimes we have to take a leap of faith and be brave to create a different life for ourselves, even when our mind casts doubts, because on the other side of that fear is magic!

Lockdown forced us to face ourselves in bigger ways than we have ever experienced. Anything that we were running away from, we had to face. Our biggest wounds triggered, we could no longer avoid them or distract ourselves with the outside world. This was a collective dark night of the soul, a great purging of all that had to be revealed, and had to go. It's easy to avoid what we need to change, fix, heal when we are constantly distracted by life and the outside world.

As a society we have learned to seek outside of ourselves, to self-medicate and distract ourselves from our own healing via the means of entertainment, drugs, sex – the list is endless. It can be extremely uncomfortable at first to sit with yourself if you're the type of person that dislikes being by themselves and needs to be around others all the time, but there is huge growth in being alone. It's in these times that I have come up with some of my best ideas or understood myself on a deeper level. If you can sit in your own company and be content then you can really start to tune into yourself and see what your true desires and needs are. If you can get to a level of being comfortable in your own company, then you can never feel lonely again.

– *Jess Lewis*

CHERUB, 35 LONDON.

Lockdown time in rhyme.
Each phase unlike the one before.
Sometimes riding waves,
sometimes resting on the shore.
Our witchy vibes could recognise
we're in the middle of a war.
A spirit battle of light and shade,
like never seen before.

Dark magic at its finest,
evil genius at its best.
The spells and symbolism
that have kept us all oppressed.
Yet, we take back our power
that they previously possessed,
when we believe our magic
and know that we are blessed.

Frustration in isolation
around each monthly moon.
We wax, we wane, we go insane,
we contract, we cocoon.

From shadow to shine,
the labyrinth of our minds.
The mystery, the mania, the spin.
Solo days and endless nights
sparks the growing light
that eternally beams from within.

We are strong and journey on
as night blends into day.
Autumn brings fresh new energy
as Summer slips away.
There are things that die
and things that leave us,
things that shed
and things that grieve us.

Yet eventually one by one,
we feel the warmth of the dawning sun.
And just like Mother Earth rebirths
during the cycles of the season.
So too can you, reset, renew,
just give yourself a reason.

Align with the circle of life
and to yourself, be true.
Let go of the old as the season fades,
and welcome in the new.

It feels like Jedi mind training
as we enter lockdown again.
When seas are rough and times are tough,
we'll learn to find our zen.

Can we seek time in stillness
as the whole world changes pace?
Use this wild ride to go deep inside,
and glide through life with grace.

This lockdown's cold, this lockdown's dark,
we can't sunbathe in the park.
So, we hibernate, and illuminate,
by firing up our inner spark.

Find new ways to self fulfil,
learn a brain engaging skill.
Music, poetry, painting, art,
create from your shining heart.

…..and it looks like we made it.
we got through this crazy year.
Let's celebrate how we played it,
we sprayed the stratosphere -
with love, faith, and frequency,
through our words, actions, and thought.
The dark forces didn't realise
we are free birds that can't be caught.

The new years come,

the old years go.
We dream, we plan,
we learn, we grow.

We reach out for stars
in the dark of night.
We rise together
in the shining light.

We keep the faith,
overcome the fear.
We welcome the potential
of this fresh new year.

We are the spiral,
we are the one,
infinitely connected.
Into you I see is me,
through you I am reflected.

A world of a million other me's
in flow of receiving and giving.
To love all as I love myself
is the key to happy living.

Awaken to what's going on,
be a free thinking detective.
Raise your frequency to see
it from a higher perspective.

Quieten the mind,
tune into body, heart and breath.
learn to let go, give in to the flow
and face your ego death.

Some days are better -
some days are worse.
Look for the blessing
instead of the curse.

Be positive, stay strong,
and get enough rest.
You can't do it all,
but you can do your best.

There is always hope for the downtrodden,
there is faith for those that believe.
There's that warm fuzzy feeling
of love, peace, and healing,
if you just open up to receive.

Do you see you can transform
when you upgrade your attitude?
Celebrate small wins,
find joy in small things,
move from lack to gratitude.

The birds are singing, the sun is blinging,
Spring is in the air.

With this fresh new weather
we stand together,
in our hearts we hold a prayer.

For a better, brighter, lighter world,
of love and harmony.
Joy for every boy and girl
in peace and unity.

In conclusion…
The only solution to the tyrannical persecution
is the people rising up in peaceful revolution.
Don't be bitter on twitter, don't smother each other
with conflict and anger - leave that to Big Brother.

Let's no longer presume
we can endlessly consume.
Slow down, breathe with nature
and the flowers will bloom.

While chaos and confusion spirals around,
we remain centred, with feet on the ground.
Go barefoot in nature to fire up your chi,
missing hugs from a human? Get that love from a tree!

Breathe in that fresh air upon Hampstead Heath.
Do coconut oil pulling to look after your teeth.
Use this time to go inside and take care of yourself.
Read that book you've been storing away on your shelf.
Trust and let go, what will be will be.

And no matter what happens..in your heart you are free.

Be kind, love each other,
treat the earth like your Mother,
keep the faith, don't buy into the political pantomime.
Walk this world with pride,
it's human nature to thrive.
Take a deep breath and remember, LOVE wins...every time.

Thank- You to Dianne, Sheryle, David, Jackie, Simon, Becca, Catarina, Lee, Richi, Nann, Freya, Vedra, Aimin, Rusty, Ben, Ruba, Andrea and John, Yvette, Fiona, Ozgita, Marco, Yaz, Ned, Katalin, Savita, Kirsty, Shira, Kay, Jonathon, Jess and Cherub for sharing all of your beautiful heartfelt words.

Without you this book would literally not exist. Thank-you for trusting your voice, and for transforming your struggles into beauty.

We are the living breathing creators of the new earth manifest.

Thanks to Lee, Tracey and Di for busting your ass with edits…

A very special message to Jackie's Dad, Richi's twins, Freya's friend Alfred, Ruba's loved ones, …my beautiful Grandma Stef and to any other blessed souls who left in 2020… May you live on in all the hearts and minds of your loved ones and future generations.

ABOUT THE AUTHOR

Lisa realised early on in life that she was not able to conform to the current system that society dictates. She embarked upon a 10 year journey around the world trying to put herself back together from a build-up of trauma in her body and mind. She began studying intensely different healing methods, ancient yogic practices & her own inner world.

Over the years, she has become fascinated with the way we can release the body from tightly held traumas through many methods; her favourites being breathwork, massage, Yoga and dance.

And also through the power of telling our stories. She has always known writing to be a powerful healer, with diaries stretching back through the years to her younger days, all stacked underneath her bed. She believes life to have a bigger meaning, that can perhaps only be understood when we look backwards.

She created her workshop, The Breath Ceremony, and has since been travelling the world with it for many years, partaking in some massive festivals' healing areas. Now she is residing in middle England and working to co-create a new healing space beside a magical lake.

Watch out for her next 2 books due to be released later this year 'Breathing Back to Life' and 'Gypsy Souls : A twin flame journey.'

Printed in Great Britain
by Amazon

59646538R00128